John Osborne Entertains

Food and Drink in The Shropshire Hills

M & K Pybus
Round Oak
Craven Arms
SY7 8HQ
keithpybus@supanet.com

First published by M & K Pybus
Copyright text ©Meg Pybus 2010
Copyright photographs
except where otherwise acknowledged
Gordon Dickins 2010

All rights reserved. No part of this publication
may be reproduced, stored in a retrieval system,
or transmitted, in any form or by any means,
electronic, mechanical, photocopying, recording
or otherwise, without the prior permission
in writing, of the publisher.

ISBN 978 0 9511387 3 1

Project Manager
Keith Pybus

Designed by
James Sherratt
Craven Design and Print Ltd

Printed by
Precision Colour Printing
Haldane, Halesfield 1
Telford, Shropshire
TF7 4QQ

Cover illustration: Gordon Dickins
Concept and art direction Catherine Pybus

John Osborne Entertains

A collection of recipes from The Hurst
cooked and eaten by the students / writers
influenced by John and Helen Osborne's favourite meals
who lived and dined from this rich Shropshire countryside.

*To the founders, trustees, volunteers and staff
of the Arvon Foundation who believe in the power of writing
to enrich our lives and even to transform them.*

John Osborne, 1986
Jane Bown / Guardian News & Media Ltd 2006

BILL OF FARE

Starters	13
The man and his food	19
The two kitchens	24
The Hurst recipes	31
The wild things	61
The writers' recipes	75
Index of recipes	91
About the authors	96

The Hurst Visitor Book

Sign here .....

....
....
....
....
....
....
....
....
....
....
....
....
....
....
....
....
....
....

"You ARE leaving on Sunday aren't you?"
Osborne embroidered cushion motto

I Propose a Toast to...

In the beginning was a simple idea, not even a title. At a meeting of the Arvon local advisory committee some four years ago, inevitably we reached that point on the agenda 'Fundraising'. Centre Director Kerry Watson suggested a cookery book. The writers attending the courses had asked for copies of the recipes to take home.

After almost thirty years on a dream country estate in North Shropshire, I had already fallen in love for a second time. The Hurst was another reminder of the heydays of country house entertaining. Earlier I had written *Under the Buttercross – Market Drayton a town of good food.* Our move to the Shropshire Hills had been a stroke of good fortune. I was starting to relive the inspirations of that book, like John and Helen coming from the south-east.

Starting to instil myself in the world of the Osbornes and The Hurst, at my desk I surrounded myself with Helen Osborne's cookery books and cuttings. Her favourites were familiar names – Elizabeth David, Jane Grigson, Eliza Acton ... Spattered pages, dog-eared, and spineless they were proof of a passion for cooking and reading.

A first concept began to emerge; Helen's favourite recipes linked to the Shropshire seasons, the produce of the kitchen garden, the Clun Valley and the Shropshire Hills. I could identify the formation of John's tastes by reading John Heilpern's biography *John Osborne A Patriot for Us.*

Still John and Helen were only ghosts.

As I began to fill in the outlines of their lives at The Hurst, a second concept arose. Sue Mercer, their housekeeper, and Andy Williams, the estate manager, were my 'confidential informers' on the daily life of the Osbornes.

The local Arvon committee are not just would-be-scribes, they have practical skills which extend to making cakes for the annual gardens event.

The Clunton Scrumpers gave us the opportunity to use our abundant apple crop, squeezed into fresh juice for the writer/visitors to The Hurst. The Marcher Apple Network helped us identify the varieties in the orchard. Diggory Kempton was instrumental in ensuring the survival of the old trees. Their offspring are now distributed over several community orchards.

Arvon celebrated 40 years of inspiring creative writing in 2008. Meanwhile the writers came and went, still needing the photocopied recipes. The book simmered and the committee began to get into its stride.

Déjàvu, John's last play, was my epiphany. In the stage directions, he brings their kitchen at The Hurst to life. I saw that I could employ the Osborne domestic kitchen and the new writers' kitchen in The Clockhouse to tell the story of food and drink in the Shropshire Hills Area of Outstanding Natural Beauty.

Years 2 and 3 rolled on, the committee listened to the latest concept and agreed all would be well 'sometime in the future'. Funding was swept under our table.

One day there was a flash from a camera.

Our good friend, Gordon Dickins, ace photographer of life in Shropshire, joined our committee. In *Shropshire Seasons, Quiet Mysteries* and *The Shropshire Hills* he had already recorded the life and landscape. Now he agreed to capture the seasonal foods from the garden, the fields and orchards. Through the lens he viewed the markets, the shops, the stalls, wherever food, particularly local, could be found.

I had drawn the Osbornes but only in part. To fill out my picture, I needed more informants. In Clun and Ludlow, London, even as far away as Crete, without the help of the following, I could not have 'dined with' the Osbornes.

George Byatt, Sue Dowell, Jean and John Gethin, Judy Harper, Ruth and Colin Mapes, Carys Palmer, Colin Pendry, Brenda and David Reid, Jay and Peter Upton, Winifred Wells and Joyce Williams.

My researches began understandably in Clun. In Clun there is one great authority on the local retailers. Frank Wells, butcher and main supplier to The Hurst, has compiled a directory of trade and commerce in Clun from the 1930s. With his help I was able to check back which shops co-existed with the Osbornes.

David Burnett of Excellent Press, Ludlow, publisher of Peter Brear's *Traditional Food in Shropshire,* inviting me to review this book, rekindled all my enthusiasm for the history of our dishes.

All my friends at Arvon: Pat Beech convinced me that the very early rough concept was worth pursuing. The local advisory committee Katie Adam, Gordon Dickins, David Kendall and Ruth Mason. Ed Collier and Paul Warwick, first Centre Directors at The Hurst were able to provide the details of everyday life with Helen as their neighbour. My great friends Kerry Watson and Peter Salmon, current Centre Directors, with whom we have tasted and toasted the produce of the Clun Valley on many happy occasions. Dan Pavitt, Centre Administrator, who links us all together.

To the very end of my researches I was receiving the nicest touches about 'life with the Osbornes' I am grateful to the Reverend Prebendary Richard Shaw - Vicar of Clun – for his champagne moment.

Four dynamic people have brought *John Osborne Entertains* to table.

My husband is a tireless driver and enthusiast, apart from his role as editor and fund-raiser, his feet are my source of detailed knowledge of the Shropshire Hills, its footpaths and wild produce. His culinary speciality is Indian food. To him I owe the dawn aroma of Mumbai throughout the house, as he mass-produced chutney.

Cath Landles, Community Officer, Shropshire Hills AONB, recognised the potential of this book for promoting sustainable development, and by encouraging us to apply for a grant she has advanced the project by at least a year.

Mark Hotchkiss of HSBC brought publishing the book to the attention of the bank as a community event. Samantha Bradford and Eleanor Almonte ensured it received backing from the West Midlands area.

To write a book you need a close-by support group. After a morning at the desk, daughter, Kate, has cleared my head on our regular afternoon walks. Simon Smith, my taster and consultant, has kept us fed whilst I cooked on paper. The house would have fallen down about my ears had I not had Nick Smith to keep everyday wear-and-tear at bay.

Last but not least – I raise my glass to the traditional breeds who have shaped both the landscape and our Sunday meals and to all the friendly and expert butchers at D.W. Wall &Son in Craven Arms.

The extract from the play DEJA VU by John Osborne published by Faber & Faber in John Osborne Plays One copyright the Arvon Foundation who have kindly granted permission.

The photograph of John Osborne on p5 copyright Jane Bown/Guardian News & Media Ltd 2006

For permission to reproduce two recipes from Shropshire Food by Karen Wallace and Norrie Davies for her painting of Mr Wells' shop on p14

The photograph of Helen Osborne on p23 by kind permission of George Byatt

The woodcut of Offa at The Hurst by Jonathan Heale on p33 with the kind permission of the artist

STARTERS

Sir Walter Scott, AE Housman, Mary Webb, EM Forster ... Clun is a very confluence of writers and their inspiration.

Anyone lucky enough to stay at The Hurst in the Clun Valley, part of this idyll of outstanding natural beauty, will have returned home with everlasting memories. Who can ever forget the first sight of snowdrops against the backdrop of the snow-clad hills, the bluebell haze of the woodlands or a spring walk up to the redwoods, catching the scent of wild garlic on the way?

Some may have savoured early summer days in the garden amidst the azaleas and rhododendrons, or gathered romantic notions under the rose arbour, mingled with the heady scent of honeysuckle.

Others pick that particular word or phrase with the first apple from the old orchard. Listening to the water trickling down The Dingle to the pool, a glimpse of zig-zagging electric blue dragon flies may have captured many a creative flow.

A chilling mystery may have evolved from listening to winter storms, whistling round the solid Georgian house. Writers' block saved waking to the sound of the woodsman's axe. Words, sentences, pages gush from this spiritual paradise.

At least as powerful as any of these memories is taste. The aroma of cooking from the Writers' Kitchen summons us to supper.

Meals at The Hurst are a celebration of place. The Clun Valley is where John Osborne and his wife Helen chose to spend their retiring years. They escaped the noise of the south-east for this grand-if-neglected rural estate set in this rich agricultural landscape. The same raw materials which had first attracted Sean Hill and the other Michelin-starred chefs to Ludlow were their daily bread - food from the Shropshire hills, the soft fertile valleys, their own fruit cages, the orchard and the still-partially-walled kitchen garden.

On their walks Lulu, Max and Mini, the Osborne dogs, introduced John to the scenes where he could 'eat the view'. To the traditional breeds of cattle and pigs and especially to the sheep which bear the names of the area, the Clun Forest, the Kerry Hill and the Shropshire. They flushed out the ubiquitous pheasants, partridges and rabbits. Later in the shops and markets these goodies would be transformed into his favourite pork and game pies.

In his biography *John Osborne A Patriot For Us* John Heilpern tells of John Osborne's special walk. "One night, we were walking along Broadway ... when he began to lean forward peculiarly like a strange version of Groucho Marx in a strong headwind. He told me it was the best way to walk, particularly over long distances, and called it "The Countryman Tramp's Walk." It had been taught to him by his eccentric grandfather. And now he taught it to me. We tried it out together, doing the Countryman Tramp's Walk along the Great White Way, and even New Yorkers, who've seen everything, looked curious as we surged past them."

Clun, Shropshire's smallest town, with a handful of shops was the source of their introduction to country traditions and local specialities. On a fine day when the beloved open-top Alvis could be risked an outing to Clun, he could be seen in *The Sun* or

chatting to Janet Davies in the newsagents. Janet gave John the odd winning tip on the horses. If it turned up he would repay her with rare perfume from London or by taking her sons out in the Alvis.

Helen's visits to Frank Wells the butcher in The Square were a countdown of the week.

STARTERS

Tuesdays his eye-catching displays of offal would tempt her to choose from the kidneys, liver, oxtail, hearts and sweetbreads which formed a tasty part of John's preference for good, honest fare. Before the weekend he enjoyed 'a nice bit of steak' and especially the succulent lamb chops or in winter slow-cooked beef casseroles from the AGA. If there was to be a large dinner party, then Frank might supply a saddle of lamb. Sundays were very traditional – the roast pork would greet friends in the dining room.

The breadth of her reading and the collection of cookery books dictated the occasional visit further afield. Ludlow market and the surrounding specialists were a Mecca. At the so-fittingly named *Farmers* in Mill Street she might be rubbing shoulders with starred-chefs Sean Hill or Claude Bosi. *The Deli on the Square* provided many of the exotics. Venison from nearby Mortimer Forest came from two of the leading butchers. If there was a problem with bread it could only have been what to choose from award-winning Price's tempting range – Ludlow Brown, several kinds of rye and every other grain. On the way home a call in to

Harry Tuffins, Craven Arms would yield packaged goods for the store cupboard, and speciality flours for home-baking.

When not dining at home, they took their friends to their discoveries amongst the local restaurants. Colin Pendry remembered seeing John Cleese at The Old Post Office in Clun. They loved The Stagg Inn at Titley. A preference endorsed by Michelin, who awarded it their very first star to a pub. Helen and John's guest Dame Maggie Smith's visit is recalled with pride. Their tastes were truly catholic. One day it might be the

15

Engine and Tender's BIG engineburgers in Broome whilst at The Jolly Frog, Leintwardine, Helen's standing order was lobster and chips.

Andy Williams, who cared for the estate, and Brian Corley, the kitchen gardener, supplied plenty of seasonal vegetables. In summer there were soft fruits, tomatoes, cucumbers and grapes from the greenhouses. The orchard at The Hurst has survived many decades. The apple varieties are typical of a Victorian orchard. The unusual Curl Tail, with no stalk but a fleshy protuberance is rare in these parts. The Victorians had a weakness for exhibitions and Howgate Wonder - now on its last legs – is an 'Exhibition apple' – a dumpling made of one of these would feed a family. A small apple press is a reminder of the time when Andy would make apple juice for the Osbornes from the crop.

On the borage, which once formed part of her herb garden, bees are busying themselves, handy for the back door - so handy for that refreshing glass of Pimm's.

Entertaining

The house was a perfect place for their lavish entertaining of old friends, actors, writers and artists. Earl Gowrie was a good friend of Helen's. Sue Mercer, the housekeeper, recalls Eileen Atkins, Edward Fox, Emily Mortimer, Dame Maggie Smith, Sylvia Simms, Ludlovians Anthony Howard and his wife Carol, the Nichols from Hopesay, Peter Bowles and his wife. It's still a place of hospitality in its new guise as writers' paradise and place for scrumptious food.

Shropshire folk are known for their hospitality – a "Shropshire do" often combined their love of a good time with a charitable purpose. Estates like The Hurst were centres of country house entertaining with tennis courts, village cricket and clay-pigeon shooting at neighbouring Hurst Mill Farm. They reached their apogee prior to World War I. In 1925 The Hurst ceased to be the centre of a large agricultural estate, reduced to the 30 acres of today. If John had chosen The Hurst as a place of withdrawal to complete the second volume of his autobiography, Helen loved people and having a Shropshire do was an important part of her life. The book has many favourite recipes from the Osborne kitchen, where Helen and John spent a good deal of their time

Although The Hurst, once THE major estate with the imposing dower house in the main street of the town, owned by the same family who controlled Clun Castle, fell on hard times, it is now enjoying a total renaissance as The John Osborne Arvon Centre. I like to feel the Osbornes supplied the bridge to this exciting future.

The idea for the book was to provide the recipes for the writers. They are all original and also cater for those with individual dietary needs. They are as cooked and eaten by the writers during their courses. They can recapture the spirit of their week at The Hurst and use the recipes at home for entertaining literary friends or book groups. To preserve something of that experience, I have kept the original quantities for 15 or more. They can easily be scaled down to more modest literary soirees.

Beyond The Hurst is the whole productive landscape of the Clun Valley and the Shropshire Hills of the agriculture and the bountiful open country. The Wild Things is a chapter which invites you to pull on your boots and explore. I hope it converts many to the joy of foraging.

The Man And His Food

John Osborne's childhood, impoverished both emotionally and physically, first shaped his taste in food. His mother, Nellie Beatrice, was a party-loving barmaid. She was not a home-lover, the comfort of husband or son was not her priority.

John's adored father died from TB in 1940. John never forgave her for neglecting him. John was only ten, a sickly child. Nellie B couldn't stand "dead and alive holes" After his father's agonising death, they moved from one small rented place to another. It was a hand-to-mouth existence, lacking the will and the facilities to cook, John's diet was fish and chips, takeaways, pies, often eaten alone whilst she was in the pub.

Wartime did not improve things. Marguerite Patten's tips would have passed Nellie by. These were hard times in the Anderson shelter listening to bombs during the Blitz. A lonely child, longing for a family atmosphere, John was often found at his friend Mickey Wall's welcoming house. In this second home he would experience sitting round a table eating proper meals.

Having suffered so many illnesses and weakened by rheumatic fever, he grew up a hypochondriac. At 14 he was sent to Belmont College in Devon, paid for from his father's contribution to the Benevolent Society. Without any knowledge of the school meals we can only deduce they would have been regular probably filling, with a good deal of "stodge". This diet seems to have transformed the puny child. He took up boxing in the school team to some effect, being expelled for punching the headmaster.

Nellie's tips from GIs paid for slap-up cream teas at the Regent Palace Hotel, whilst she enjoyed her G & T. For the 15-year-old John a real treat was fish and chips and a cigar at J Lyons 'Troc' in Piccadilly.

From the age of 18 he was a vegetarian for ten years, converted by Stella Linden, his first lover. For seven years he toured the smaller repertory circuit as actor in minor parts and as assistant stage manager. £3 a week breakfast, tea and supper in rundown seaside towns may have been where he developed the passion for eels in every form.

Success

His plays Look Back in Anger and The Entertainer, his screenplays, but above all his share in the profits of Woodfall Films made him very rich, He could afford to live off the high hog, but he still preferred good plain fare. Steak and kidney pudding, bacon sandwiches, kippers, huge mushrooms, lamb stew, bacon and beans, bread and cheese, gherkins, cold meats, German sausages (he overlooked their nationality), cold mussels, eels cooked or jellied, bread and butter pudding were some of his favourites.

Home cooking at last

Helen Dawson, his fifth wife, at last gave him the love and stability of a real home both at Christmas Place and at The Hurst. A fiery Geordie she shone for John like a bright star. One of his nicknames for her was *Twink*. She had so much in common with John, with her humour and wit having been one of the best drama critics of her time. Helen believed that God's majesty was manifest in The Word. Both hated the abandonment of the Book of Common Prayer and the King James's Bible.

The Man And His Food

The move from Christmas Place, Edenbridge was designed to release capital to pay off pressing debts to the tax people and the bank. This sensible solution went out the windows of The Hurst a twenty-room 1812 house in the Clun Valley, Shropshire. John had chosen one of Housman's 'quietest places under the sun.'

They arrived in Shropshire with a menagerie, two horses, two donkeys and three dogs. These dogs were the children they never had. Sometimes they joined in uninvited. Taking a pre-dinner drink in the drawing room, you might be greeted by Helen head-in-hands announcing that the dogs had 'tried your dinner.' You could hear the sound of plates being licked. Everything could be solved with a glass and a good meal. There were hours spent together in the womb of the kitchen, their acerbic wit writhing in the smoke of their cigarettes and cigars

Sue Mercer, the housekeeper, lived in the cottage adjoining the big house. The kitchen doors conveniently interconnecting for Sue and Helen to discuss meals for the day round the kitchen table. Sue remembers Helen, glass in hand, preparing the next day's meals to slow cook in the AGA. At home they might entertain formally. She loved entertaining and was not fazed by large dinner parties or weekend cooking. Ed Collier, one of the first Arvon Centre Directors at The Hurst, remembers her as "a wonderful and generous ... host." The Uptons recalled the sun streaming through the large windows of the dining room at The Hurst. Helen took pride in her table layouts. But just as their tastes ranged from the burger to lobster, you might be invited to a supper in the kitchen for bangers and mash.

Combined with caring for The Hurst, Helen continued with book reviews for The Spectator and the Sunday Telegraph. Sue Mercer remembers her study "stuffed with books." Her review copies are now scattered around the bookshelves of good friends in Clun. Cookbooks could also be presents. Jay Upton and Judy Harper treasure Helen's gifts – The Ivy and Kitchen Essays by Agnes Jekyll. Other books from John and Helen would arrive in quantity for Jay's charity book fairs.

"It is not true that drink changes a man's character. It may reveal it more clearly."
John Osborne

In blazer and a boater, waving a cigarette, holding a glass of champagne, John relished playing the genial host, the country squire at play. They continued the tradition of Edenbridge theatrical parties but on a less lavish scale, for their visiting friends and locals. The fire brigade was invited to their annual bonfire.

Champagne was their ubiquitous love. Employees of Tanners, Shropshire's leading wine merchants, recall John as a regular customer, ordering large quantities of their house champagne. Perhaps these Tanner's deliveries lie in the deep tranquillity of The Hurst pool. When the Osbornes sold Christmas Place, the buyers drained the lake only to excavate a huge wreckage of bottles.

Rather than tea with the vicar, John extended to the cloth the same lifestyle as he would to his friends from the theatre. The Reverend Prebendary Richard Shaw - Vicar of Clun – recalls: "My one memory of John Osborne's hospitality is of champagne being always available in the kitchen - He used to open the gardens of The Hurst in aid of St George's Church, when the azaleas were in full flower - in preparation for the "Open Day" - John would give me a tour of the gardens - they were wonderful - then it was into the kitchen for champagne - it did not seem to matter what time of the day it was - generous hospitality was always on offer!"

The Gang of Four or the DHSS

John nicknamed a group of four eminent local wives the WOWS – the washed-out wives. One day in 1989 the four women came together for lunch at the house of Sue Dowell in Clun. It was a success and went on well into the night. A month later they came together at The Hurst to celebrate Helen's birthday. Thereafter they wined, dined and swapped recipes in each other's houses. The dates were a priority in their social calendar. If there was a clash with another date, they would always say "I'm going to the DHSS."

"I don't like competitive cooking," Helen used to say, as she served her delicious homemade fish cakes to the DHSS. D [iana Forester] H [elen] S [ue Dowell] S [elena Joyce Williams]

Helen alone

She wrote, for The Sunday Telegraph, about widowhood: "There are no road maps in this blasted landscape. When a marriage of unselfconscious mutual dependence is silenced, sliced off, you are on your own as never before." Helen supplemented her income from John's royalties, by writing for The Telegraph some highly acerbic and well-informed reviews of theatrical biographies, trying to "cock a snook at humbug at all times, as he did". She once appended the words: "The fee from this article is going to the Helen Osborne Survival Fund."

A Debt Repaid

Amongst the guests at their dinner parties had been 'Grey Gowrie', Alexander Patrick Greysteil Ruthven, 2nd Earl of Gowrie. After politics and Minister of the Arts, he was Chairman of Sotheby's and of the Arts Council of England. At the Arts Council he was responsible for allocating funds from the national lottery. This fund was to solve Helen's financial problems and to provide the Arvon Foundation with a third base for their courses in creative writing. An Arts Council Capital Lottery Grant provided the means to acquire The Hurst whilst guaranteeing Helen's continued residence there.

The John Osborne Arvon Centre at The Hurst was underway. From 1999 until 2003, Helen struggled with 'having the builders in'. With Helen's involvement, the first Centre Directors were appointed. Ed Collier and Paul Warwick had a background in theatre. They shared many interests with her. Pat Beech, chairman of the local Advisory Committee, recalled Ed and Paul meeting the estate manager Andy Williams for the first time "It was another occasion for the champagne to flow."

The new venture was opened by Dame Maggie Smith in March 2003, and Helen served on the committee. She contributed ideas enthusiastically, and - rather more than her husband would have done - enjoyed having people constantly round her. From the fresh start Helen was entertaining. The Arvon local advisory committee was offered a light lunch of salads from the garden, local bread and cheeses. Joyce Williams can still picture 'vast plates of attractively composed salads, which I wished I could emulate, but I never dared."

Helen's love of company blossomed anew; trips to London, 'a life-line,' to stay with Maggie Smith, the races with Viscount Windsor. Her local circle widened. Judy Harper, who remembers dinner parties together, became a great friend. Diane Davis was brought in to cater for a number of her parties. She dined with Brenda and David Reid in Crete five or six times.

When the history of Ludlow's gastronomic revolution comes to be written, it must not omit The Cookhouse at Bromfield. Norman Swallow had swapped Waltons in Chelsea for Shropshire's first roadhouse or gastro pub. The Cookhouse used to be a pub, the Clive Arms. The menu appealed to Helen's taste from brasserie to transport caff - steak-and-kidney pie, bangers and mash, croque monsieur; a simple selection of something for everyone. Norman and George Byatt organised a picnic to Harlech beach. Helen refused at the cliff descent. To entice her down the path they waved a bottle of champagne. Whilst the others swam, Helen imbibed. Helen would combine work and pleasure – reviewing the latest videos was an occasion for supper with Norman and George, even if the review passed over that it sent them to sleep.

Claude Bosi, later to take Mayfair by storm, had opened Hibiscus to rave reviews and more stars. Helen welcomed his sophisticated Clun Valley Whimberry Clafoutis. Also in Ludlow were the 'Sketchley meals' with friends, Prue Bellak or Mirabel Osler, when Helen collected her dry-cleaning.

As Helen became more frail she was fortunate in her friends. Ed and Paul were always on the spot. Andy and Ben Walden were her life-support. Joyce Williams of neighbouring Hurst Mill Farm was with her to the end. She remembers Helen's last day at The Hurst. "She was sitting in her kitchen with the dogs by the AGA, pale, weak and chesty. Andy had to carry her to the car, which took her to the hospital. She died the next day."

She died 12 January 1994 and was buried next to her beloved husband in St George's churchyard, Clun.

courtesy of George Byatt

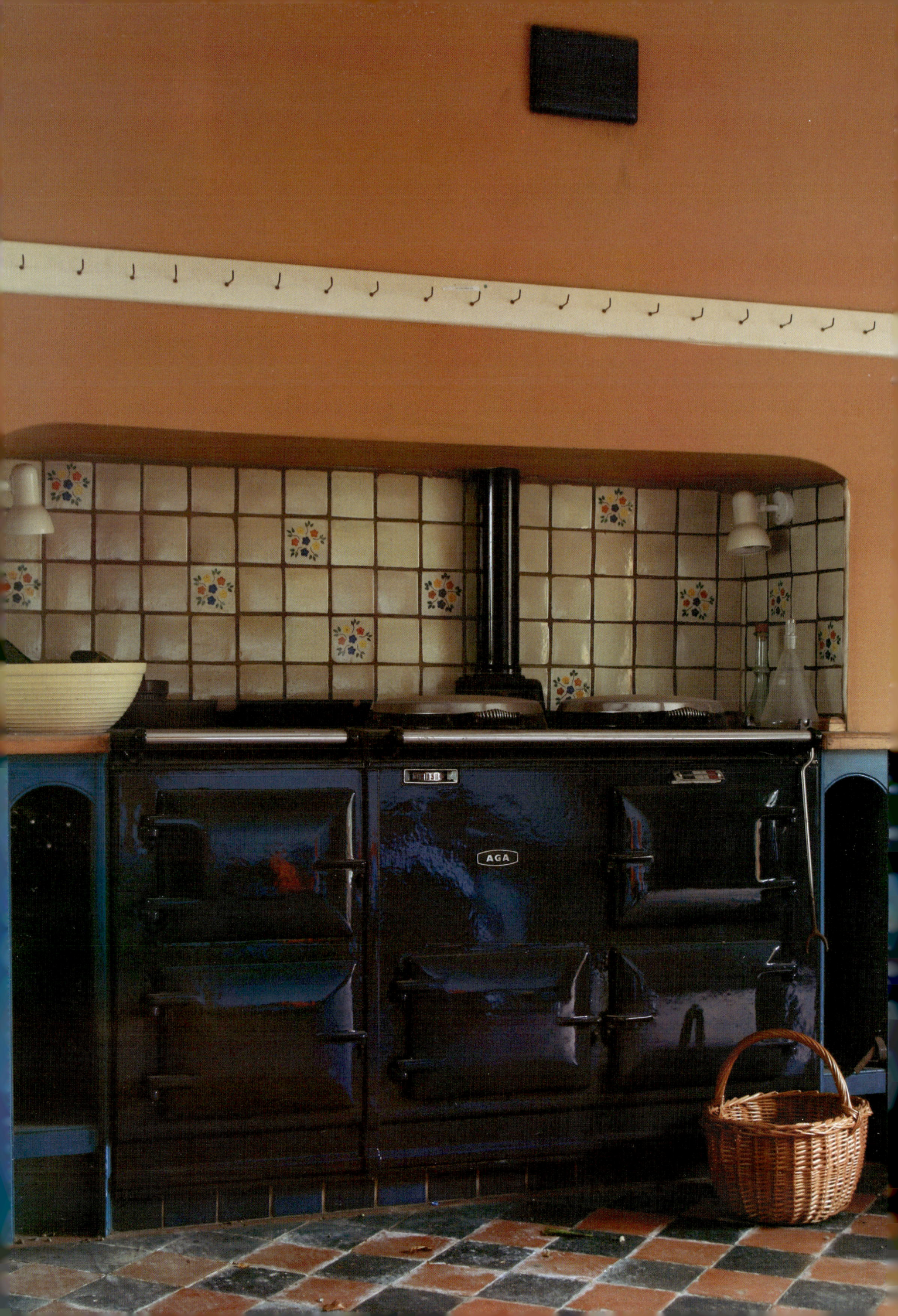

Two Kitchens

Helen's old kitchen with its vast AGA contrasts with the purpose-built kitchen, where the Arvon students cook today.

In his last play **Déjàvu** John draws upon The Hurst kitchen for his inspiration. The curtain rises on Jimmy Porter and a very different set of characters, but this lovingly detailed domestic scene is The Hurst.

The Midlands ... The large kitchen of a country house of the kind sometimes advertised as "a minor gentleman's residence". The kitchen itself retains its original farmhouse appearance of a working place at the heart of the building... It is possibly the oldest part of the house with the original stone flags from an earlier period gleaming, leading off to a butler's pantry, rooms for hanging game and preparing other fruits of the countryside. A few ancient hooks hang down from the ceiling and a huge Aga dominates one side of the stage.

All this workmanlike air of practicality has been modified in the interests of comfort, without too much emphasis on glossy Country Living... It has rather evolved as a sitting room and kitchen, a place for talk and conviviality.

A warm glow from the Aga niche gives out a comforting light from its engine-room sparkling surface. A large empty dog basket with its scatter of hairy blankets spilling out from it stands besides the stove, together with a sporting gun and cartridge belt. Upstage, large, floor-length windows look out to a distant park-like landscape with hills of pasture and a forest beyond. The walls of its cupboards and discreet units are covered with old postcards. A few sporting prints and posters decorate other walls. A wooden, rough table, which serves for both dining and working, dominates the centre area, flanked by a couple of extremely bright and comfortable old armchairs There is also a seasoned bench and rocking chair, a Windsor chair or two.

It was not all Country Living cosy; a strange enigmatic note came to my attention in one of the cookbooks; on one side 'Firelighters and Do Lights'. In contrast on the other 'You make my life bleaker.' Family deaths associated with December could afflict John with bouts of depression. John would trudge the hills with the dogs, fearful of his flickering light. Helen sat amidst her friends, the cookbooks and the blue AGA. Judy Harper remembers the scene with "two wooden mask-like parakeets hanging on either side of the AGA, you couldn't miss them they were so prominent." *All this workmanlike air of practicality has been modified in the interests of comfort, without too much emphasis on glossy Country Living. ... It has rather evolved as a sitting room and kitchen, a place for talk and conviviality.*

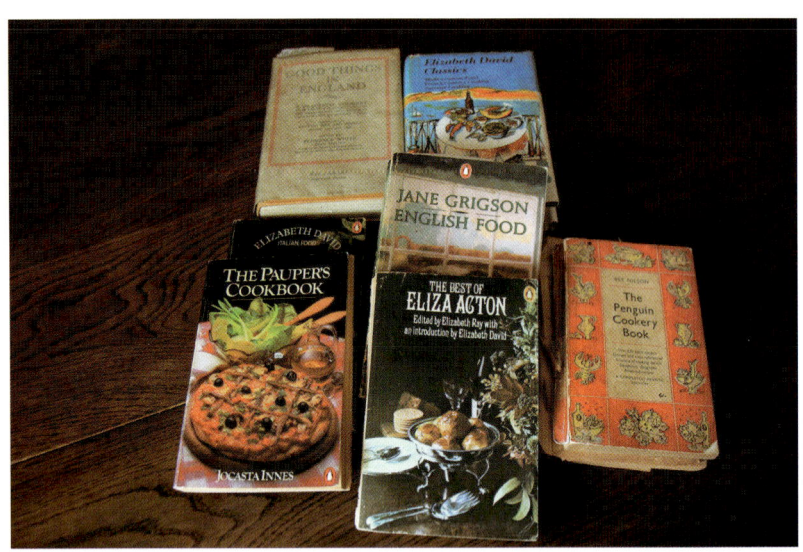

John's favourite meals were classic English fare, plain food like fish and chips, steak and kidney pie, whereas Helen's tastes were more refined. Helen introduced him to specialities adapted from her well-used favourite cook books. Sue has retained many Jane Grigson, [with whom she shared her origins in the North-east] Elizabeth David, Jocasta Innes, Eliza Acton, Bee Nilson. For the AGA recipes The Country Range Cookbook by Carol Bowen. Even in the 1990s Helen's repertoire did not stand still; Gary Rhodes, Two Fat Ladies, The River Cafe Cookbook were adopted.

THE WRITERS' KITCHEN

The Arvon creed is that cooking for fellow writers is a generous act of spirit. The act of preparing and cooking food is a good mental release and a different form of creativity. The small 'task-force' enhances group cooperation, organisation and friendship.

Without dreaming of taking on the redoubtable John Osborne, I like to imagine the stage directions for the modern kitchen – it is suitably wordy.

"a large sign PLEASE WASH HANDS BEFORE HANDLING FOOD disfigures the stainless steel fridge. More instructions; chopping boards must stick to their symbolic colour codes: raw meat is red, raw fish is blue, salads and fruit are green, dairy white, vegetables brown and cooked meat yellow.

To lighten the mood magnetic fridge words are jumbled awaiting the next kitchen poets.

Opposite more labels on the cupboards and drawers. Top left wheat-free flour, rice flour, gluten-free, dairy-free, sugar-free; a whole free world. Oat milk and soya milk that we may remain allergy free.

More signs Cutlery, Cups, Jugs, Knives. A trolley in the manner of a butcher's block protrudes from the far end of the kitchen.

On the blackboard the menu *Spinach & Ricotta Lasagne + Fruit Crumble*

Enter Kerry, a Centre Director. She moves back and forth from the pantry offstage with large boxes of cheese, giant milk cartons, huge bags of spinach, a basket of apples.

Two Kitchens

Somewhat later a young blonde-haired woman enters, followed by two slightly-built women. They are reporting for culinary duties. They regard the laden trolley with apprehension. A dark-haired smiling woman bustles in and confidently dons her apron.

The Centre Director extracts recipes from the drawer marked Recipes. She reads the orders out loud, at the same time swishing a large fleet of vessels from the cupboards: two deep stainless-steel tub-like pans, a battery of knives for chopping veg and fingers, a whirling dervish of a whisk, an enormous archaic aluminium colander and a food processor from the pantry.

Her tone changes and becomes more inviting as she demonstrates making the sauce, wilting the spinach, layering the lasagne; the flavour symphony reaches its climax with the Shropshire Blue.

"Crumble everyone knows how."

Kerry leaves the scene. The real team-building can begin.

Ruth who has 'A' Levels, and once worked in a bakery, offers to do the gluten-free dish. Her partner is a vegetarian. Florence and Hannah have both cooked at home and learned the old-fashioned way from their mothers. Sammy works hard in her job, but would never buy processed or ready-meals. She loves to cook whenever she can.

As the scene ends Sammy is stirring and vigorously whisking the sauce round the deep, deep pot whilst Florence and Hannah battle with the tiny holes of the antique colander which are resisting the passage of the wilted spinach.

Same scene – an hour later. Enter a tall athletic-looking man, Peter, the other Centre Director. He has been to the station to collect the guest speaker. Ruth is peeling apples for the crumble.

Exit Peter with Florence and Hannah to pick blackcurrants in the fruit cages to combine with the apples.

Same scene two hours later. The kitchen is empty except for cooking utensils strewn around. Noises and good smells off – glasses clink, laughter...

This performance is repeated nightly from Tuesday to Friday with a changing menu and students in the roles of cooks. Kerry and Peter exchange roles.

Hurst Recipes

SPRING

Provençale leg of lamb
Chicken breasts in ginger wine
Trout recipes from a Clun angler
Beetroot and orange soup

Rhubarb Fool
Boozy bananas
Virgin Mint Julep

O the mountain is the sweeter
But the valley is the fatter
And so we deem it meeter
To carry off the latter
     Border Reiver song

South Shropshire's fortunes were earned on the backs of the sheep. It was the medieval wool trade which paid for Stokesay Castle. The succulent cuts of the traditional breeds like the Clun Forest or the Kerry Hill and Shropshire won over the Osbornes to lamb. Jane Grigson advises "for ... high-class butchery it is wise to go to an experienced man of mature years, and if his father was a butcher before him, so much the better." The Osbornes' supplier, Frank Wells, fulfilled her prescription entirely.

At The Hurst along the little stream between the two pools of the Dingle even the snowdrops are outshone by the display [and aroma] of the wild garlic.

Provençale Leg of Lamb

about 1.7 kg./ 4lb leg of lamb
Salt and freshly ground pepper
1 tbsp butter
2 cloves garlic or in season wild garlic
3 tbsp finely chopped parsley
700g/ 1½lbs potatoes
275ml/ ½pt chicken stock

Season loin of lamb with salt and pepper. Butter a casserole or gratin dish to fit leg of lamb. Rub with garlic.
Peel and slice potatoes fairly thickly. Place in overlapping layers in bottom of dish. Add salt and pepper. Chop rest of garlic and sprinkle over potatoes with finely chopped parsley. Place lamb on top and pour over chicken stock. Roast in a slow oven 325 F. 170C. Gas 3 for 1¼ - 1½ hours, less if you like it pink. *Magazine cutting found with Helen's recipe books.*

Chicken Breasts in Ginger Wine

Helen loved her books but she was no slave to them. She created many of her own variations, especially where a dash of alcohol might improve the flavour.

Organic or free range, neither Helen nor I would use anything else. Whether farmers' markets or supermarket this area has plenty of local suppliers.

4 chicken breasts
1 tbsp flour
Salt and pepper
40g/1½ oz butter
1 tbsp oil
½ fennel bulb, finely sliced
5 tbsp ginger wine
2 tbsp dry white wine
1 tbsp chives
Juice of ½ lemon
150ml/1¼ pint single cream

With a rolling pin beat the breasts until thin. Season the flour with salt and pepper. Dip both sides of the chicken in the flour.

Heat the butter and oil in a frying pan. Cook the chicken breasts until lightly browned on both sides, about 5-7 minutes. Remove from the pan and keep warm.

Add the sliced fennel to the pan and fry for 2 minutes, stirring frequently. Add the ginger wine, stir and cook for 1 minute until reduced slightly. Reduce to a gentle heat before adding the lemon juice and cream, stirring constantly, until the sauce thickens. Add the chives.

Garnish with sprigs of fresh fennel and serve at once.

Hurst Recipes

The Clun runs a few hundred yards from the kitchens of The Hurst. Fresh trout were closer to hand. Andy Williams had stocked the pool with rainbow trout "a mixture of little ones to half-pounders, which grew to three to four pounds." He was always ready to take out his rod for John and Helen, but admitted to me that Helen could sometimes set him reeling. "One day she said could I have 10 trout for a barbeque."

Trout from the River Clun
From a Clun angler

4 trout
110g/4ozs butter
$^1/_2$ tsp lemon juice
1 tbsp flour
2 tsps chopped parsley
Salt & pepper

"Clean and wash the beauties." Dry and roll them in seasoned flour. Heat 75g/3ozs butter and fry the fish gently for 10-15 minutes, turning once. Put on a warm dish, sprinkle with parsley and lemon juice, add 25g/1oz butter to the hot butter in the pan, mix well and pour over the fishes.

From *A Taste Of Clun* 1981

Offa at The Hurst, woodcut courtesy of Jonathan Heale

Beetroot & Orange Soup

Offa, their last Springer spaniel, took after his Osborne master and mistress. Sue Mercer recalls him appearing from the kitchen with ruby-red muzzle after scoffing the beetroot.

Serves: 4

450g/1lb fresh beetroot
900ml/30 fl oz vegetable stock
Juice and grated rind of 3 fresh oranges (or 200ml/7fl oz fresh orange juice)
$^1/_4$ tsp ground coriander
$^1/_4$ tsp ground cinnamon
1 bay leaf

33

Scrub the beetroot and chop off the roots and stalks.
Either chop the beetroot finely or grate them.
Put the beetroot in a soup pan with the vegetable stock, orange rind (if using) and bay leaf. Simmer gently for 20 minutes, until the beetroot is soft.
Add the spices and orange juice. Remove the bay leaf.
You can either serve it whole or liquidise it until smooth.

Tish Dockerty

Rhubarb Fool

Fools are a classic English dessert made with any soft fruit. If frozen, they can also be made into ice-cream.

Delicate forced rhubarb is a premature taste of spring. Though a vegetable, it anticipates that refreshing taste of the soft fruits to come.

450g/1lb trimmed forced rhubarb
2 tbsp water
100g/4oz caster sugar
275ml/$^1/_2$ pt double cream

Rinse the rhubarb and cook it gently in the water until soft. Add sugar.
Beat the cream in a separate bowl. Add to the mixture.
Blend in a liquidiser or, for ice-cream, freeze in a polythene container.

Serve in glass dishes with Boudoir biscuits.

Boozy Bananas

Fans of this favourite of Helen's might have been puzzled by the earlier teetotal version, Caught-short Pudding, which she submitted for the *Clun Valley Sampler,* so here's one she 'adjusted' for private consumption.

6 bananas
Juice of a lime
50g/2oz Demerara sugar
Pinch of nutmeg
¼ tsp ground cinnamon
50g/2oz butter
4 tbsp dark rum

Butter an oven-proof baking dish. Peel the fruit. Place in the dish and sprinkle with lime juice. Mix the nutmeg, cinnamon and sugar and shake over the fruit. Cut small cubes of butter and distribute evenly over the bananas. Place under a hot grill, basting occasionally until the bananas are golden.

Warm the rum in a small saucepan, pour over the bananas and light.

Virgin Mint Julep

From April into May, The Hurst herb garden zings back to life. Bees busy on the borage remind me of Helen, picking the pretty blue flowers, decoration for the Pimm's.

Mint has many guises. Less celebrated in this country than in the southern states of the US, it makes a refreshing drink with friends on the terrace in the sweltering heat of Shropshire. This version without the Bourbon is especially good with eau-de-cologne mint.

Large handful of mint leaves
175g/ 6oz caster sugar
3 bottles dry ginger ale
1 can pineapple juice
Juice of 4 lemons
Ice

Wash the mint. Bruise. Place in a basin to suffuse with the sugar, pineapple juice and the lemon juice. Cover and leave for a few hours. Strain into a tall jug or pitcher.
Add the ginger ale and ice, thin slices of lime or lemon.

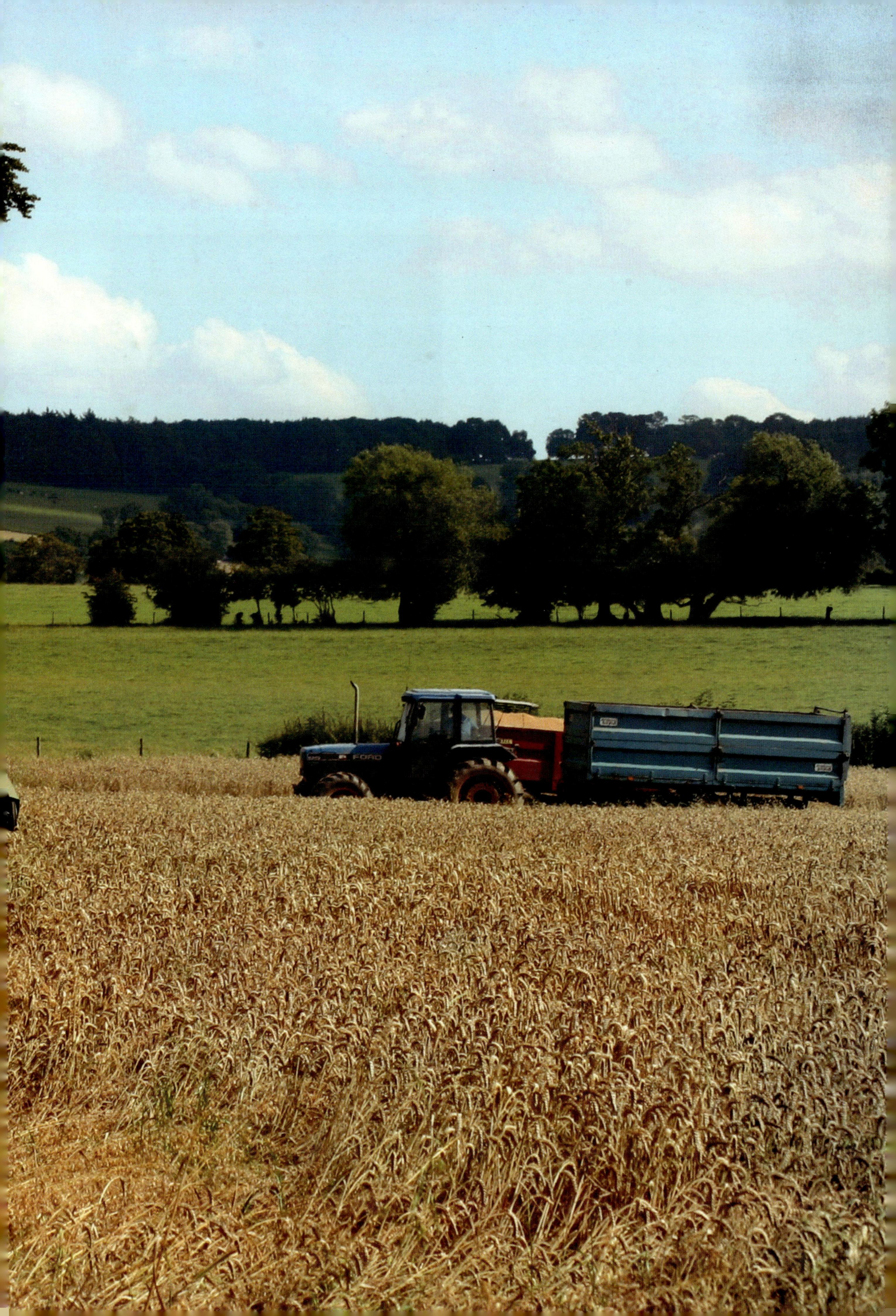

SUMMER

Roast duckling with honey
Savoury Meatballs.
Old Mother Osborne's Tomato Ketchup
Salmon en papillotte
Midsummer Magic

Wimbledon Sorbet
Blackcurrant and Gooseberry Snow

Roast Duckling with Honey

4-5lb/1.8kg-2.25kg oven-ready duckling
2-3 tbsp runny honey
1 tbsp boiling water
1 onion
1 stick celery
1 carrot
3 sprigs parsley

Remove giblets [if included] and place in a pan with onion, celery, carrot and parsley bring to the boil and simmer for a couple of hours. In the absence of giblets, use chicken stock cube.

Rub the skin of the duck with salt and prick all over. Place in a roasting tin and add 2 tbsp of cold water. Put in the oven 180C, 350F Gas 4. Allow 25 minutes per lb / 55 minutes per kilo. Half an hour before cooking is completed, pour off most of the duck fat and water. Mix the honey with the boiling water. Brush the bird with this mixture several times. Return to the oven, cook for half an hour or so until it is golden.

Make the gravy by adding 1dsp of flour to the fat residue in the tin. Stir in well over heat and add the stock slowly. A dash of gravy browning will heighten the colour.

Serve with fresh peas and new potatoes.

Savoury Meatballs

Meat balls are popular and universal, easy and can be varied with different sauces and go well with pasta, rice or potatoes. Also good eaten cold on sticks for picnics or party snacks. This recipe would be delicious with Helen's celebrated tomato sauce.

450g/1lb. sausage meat or minced steak
1 beaten egg
1 onion
1 tbsp fresh thyme (if dried use 1tsp)
Salt and pepper.
2 slices bread

Grate onion into minced beef. Soak bread in water. Squeeze out and crumble into meat. Mix in thyme. Add beaten egg, salt and pepper. Squeezing ingredients together for a smooth mixture. Form into balls. Place on a greased baking sheet and bake 220C. 425F. gas7 for 15 - 20 minutes.

Magazine cutting, no date

Old Mother Osborne's Tomato Ketchup

Helen's housekeeper Sue Mercer said this was a winner, so here is an interpretation of her recipe gleaned from her well-used Eliza Acton (first published 1845) and Mrs Beeton's Family Cookery.
Eliza calls it *Bottled tomatoes* or *Tomato Catsup.* Mrs Beeton's original of 1885 has the boring title *Tomato sauce for Keeping.* However the revised edition has the exotic name *Tomato Chow Chow* in the section pickles and chutneys all influenced from the new exciting Indian cuisine.

6 large tomatoes,
1 onion,
1 green pepper finely chopped,
1 clove garlic,
2 tbsps brown sugar,
1 tbsp salt,
275ml/$^1/_2$ pint vinegar,
a small quantity of cayenne may be used.

Peel and chop the onion finely. Blanch the tomatoes, remove the skins and slice finely. Place the onion and tomatoes in a casserole pan, add the finely chopped pepper, garlic, sugar, salt and vinegar, and cook in a slow oven until tender. Alternatively simmer in a stewing pan until soft, then sieve before bottling. This makes a finer sauce. When cold put in small jars or in wide-necked bottles and cover.

Salmon En Papillote

Once upon a time wild salmon were plentiful both in the rivers Severn and Wye. This is the king of the river fish, which spends most of its life at sea, but returns to its native river to spawn.

Helen owned a majestic salmon kettle, but nowadays we use a wrapping of foil to keep it moist in the oven. They are best served on a long serving dish decorated with cucumber and lemons. This dish would have been a perfect centre piece for The Hurst country house parties. Helen and John left Edenbridge with a reputation for parties. Their photograph album shows them living it up in the grounds with many celebrities.

So to prepare this delicate fish "cooked in a bag", prepare the foil as follows.
Cut up enough foil to enclose it loosely and enough extra for two straps if the fish is very heavy and long.

900g – 1.35kg/2-3lb salmon
4 – 6 tbsp white wine
Mixed herbs
Butter

Brush with melted butter. Sprinkle with sea salt and pepper. Place on a baking sheet with foil underneath. Pour over 4-6 tablespoons of white wine and put a lump of butter mixed with herbs inside the fish. Fold the foil fairly loosely round the fish and twist together.
Bake at 180C/350F/ gas4 for 40 -50 minutes.

Veggie Magic

This vegetarian stir-fry dish is a superb way to enjoy summer vegetables.
Helen used the abundant supplies from The Hurst garden.

450g/1lb courgettes
350g/12 oz mange-tout peas
1 yellow pepper
6 spring onions
1 red pepper
Clove garlic
2.5cm/1 in. fresh root ginger
4-5 tbsp oil
50g/2oz salted cashew nuts
3 tbsp lemon juice
4 level tbsp clear honey.
Cooked pasta or egg noodles

Thinly slice courgettes, top and tail mange-tout, cut peppers into finger length strips. Chop spring onions. Peel and finely chop ginger and garlic.

Heat 2 tablespoons oil in a wok or large non-stick sauté pan. Sauté spring onions with the courgettes for 2-3 minutes stirring occasionally until soft but keep some bite. Remove with a slotted spoon to a large bowl. Add mange -tout and peppers to the pan and sauté for 2-3 minutes stirring occasionally. Return courgettes, plus nuts, ginger and garlic, honey and lemon. Serve with cooked pasta or noodles tossed in olive oil, lemon juice and black pepper.

Wimbledon Sorbet

Helen was fond of watching Wimbledon on the telly whilst shelling peas and hulling strawberries. Sorbets, or water ices, were her favourite ways of using the delicious summer fruits brought in from the garden.

900g/ 2lb strawberries.
225g/8oz sugar.
Juice of 1/2 lemon
Juice of 1/2 orange
150ml/ 1/4 pt water

Mash strawberries through a sieve, add lemon and orange juice. Boil sugar and water for 5 minutes.

Cool and add to strawberry mixture. Freeze and stir occasionally to prevent ice crystals.

Blackcurrrant Gooseberry Snow

The soft fruit cages of The Hurst yielded a fine crop of currants and gooseberries. A well-thumbed page from one of her books, yellowed by frequent use, suggested to me this would be an annual visit.

1.2 litre /2 pints blackcurrants and gooseberries
110 g/ 4ozs caster sugar.
150ml/$^{1}/_{4}$ pint water
25g/1oz butter

For the meringue -
2 eggs
1$^{1}/_{2}$ tbsp caster sugar

Stew the berries with the sugar and water till soft. Sieve, while still warm add the butter and mix well.

Separate the whites and yolks. Beat the yolks and stir into the fruit puree when it cooled slightly. Pour into a pie dish and cook in a moderate oven 180C 350F gas4, for about 20 minutes or until the mixture has set.

Take out of the oven and while it cools whisk the egg whites, adding the sugar a little at a time, until stiff. When the meringue becomes 'glossy', spread it over the berry custard and bake at 140C 275F, gas2 for about 20 minutes until set.

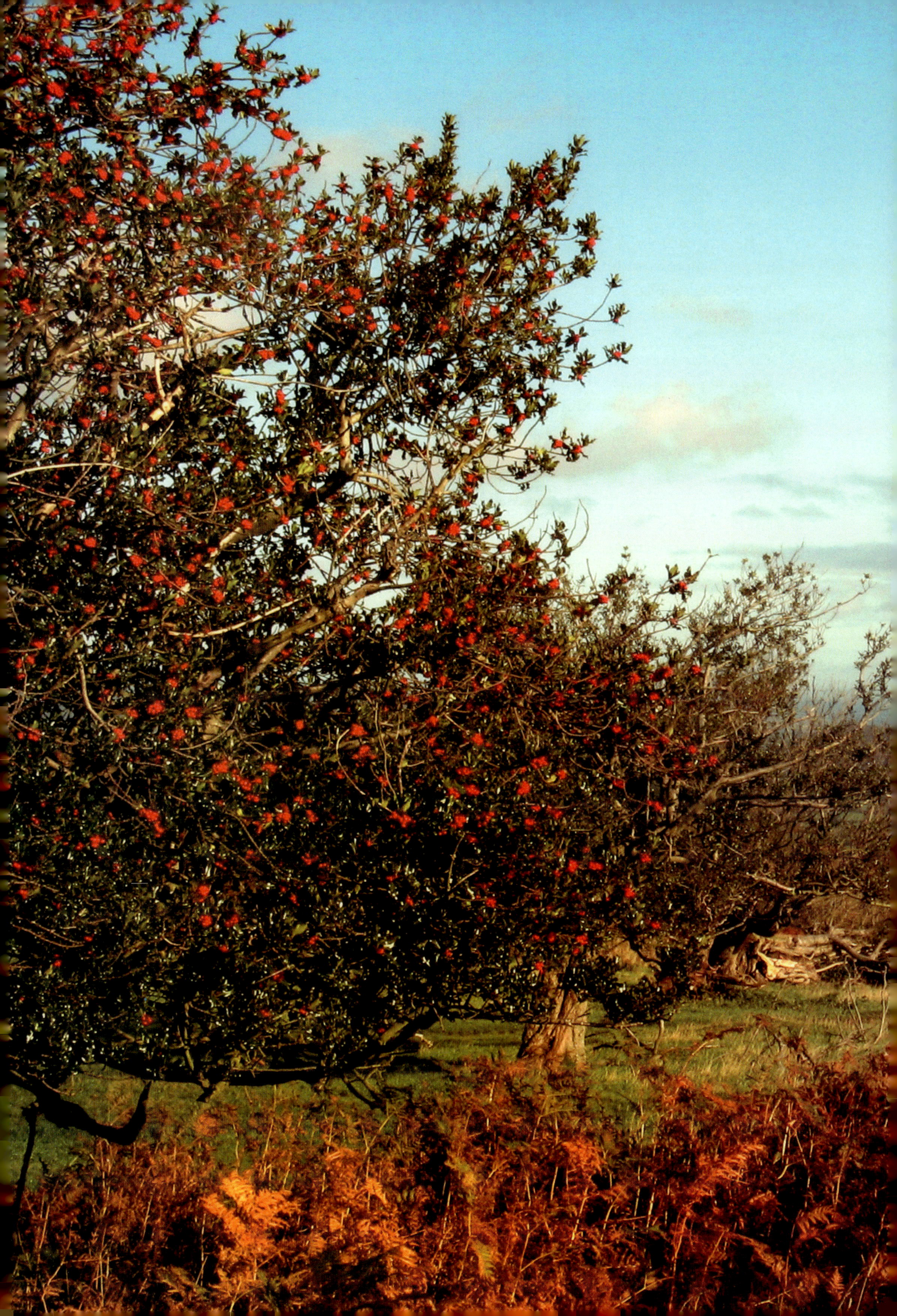

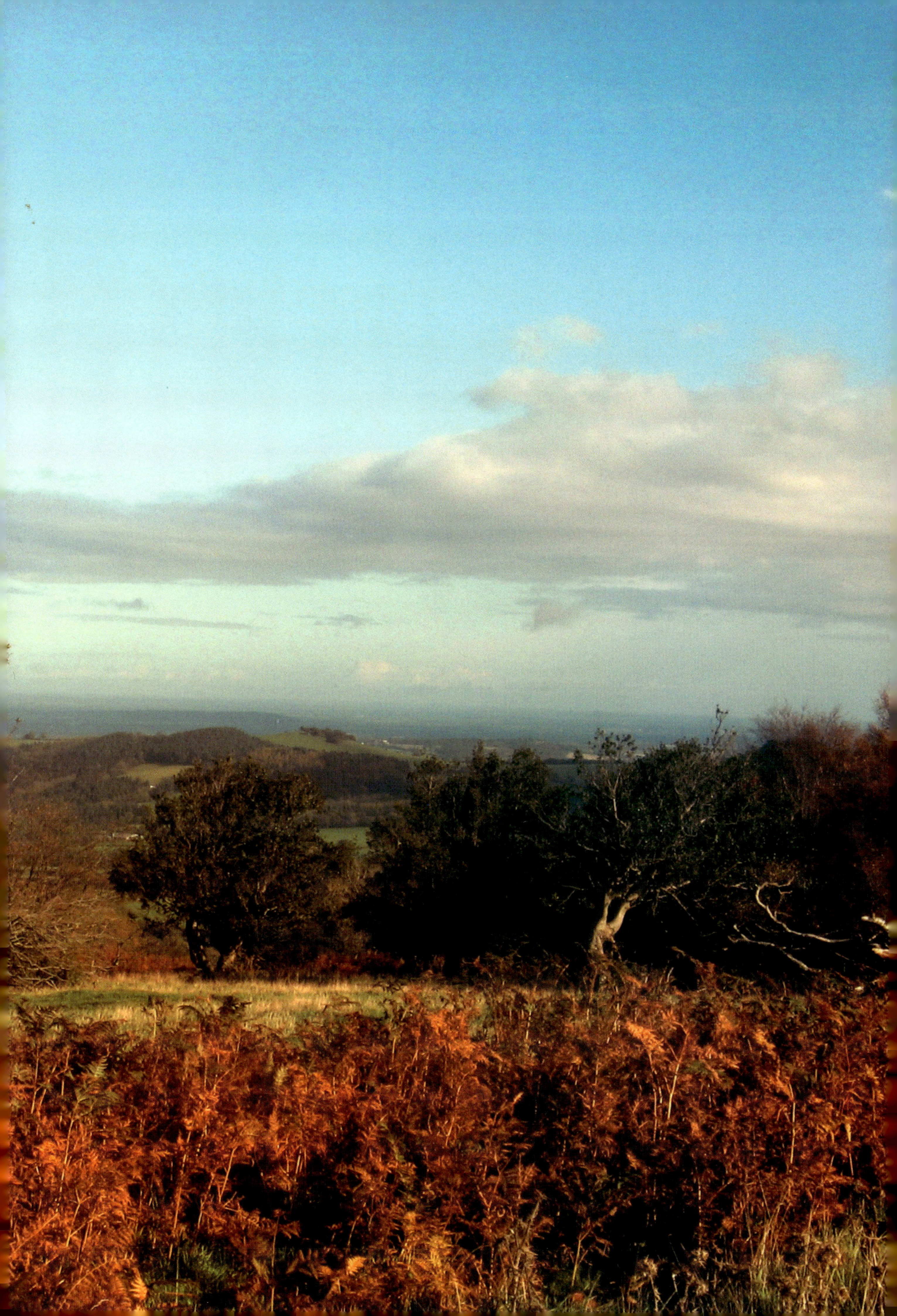

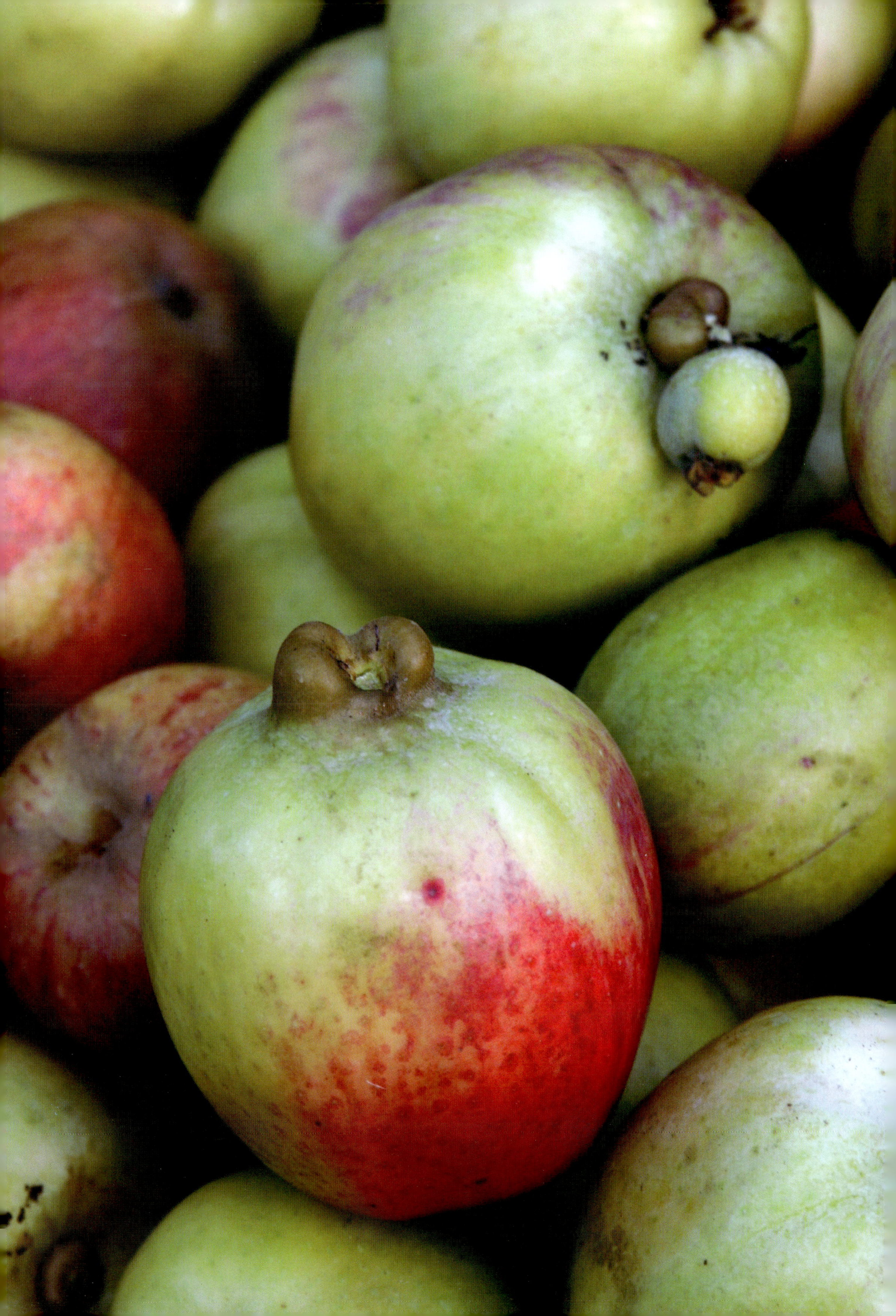

AUTUMN

Casserole of pheasant
Venison steaks with port and rowan jelly
Red cabbage
Shropshire Fitchet pie
Clive of India's apple chutney

Damson Sauce with ice cream

Blackberry and Apple Dumplings

When John and Helen arrived at The Hurst they found they had inherited a vintage orchard. The Arvon Foundation has begun the task of identifying the varieties. The Marchers Apple Network helped them – Curl Tail, Howgate Wonder, Carlisle Codlin are typical of a Victorian orchard.

"We picked all the apples in the morning and arrived at Clunton Village Hall with loads more than we feared – the Curl Tail has had another good year.

The Clunton Scrumpers had received an apple macerator and juice press from the Shropshire Hills AONB under the Blue Remembered Hills grant scheme. It was a lovely sight and smell to see this small community getting together to press the apple flesh – some people had a couple of bags from their garden and we had the produce of at least half a dozen still productive trees.

When we arrived the juice was just a trickle ... soon we were in the flow and The Hurst's crop advanced slowly towards the machines, which were manned entirely by volunteers including a farmer with apple cheeks from that wine-dark almost black variety.

Finally we were up. The first consignment went into the macerator – out comes the pulp into the bucket, to be scooped into the layers of cloth and frames of the press. Then, accompanied by a feeling of indescribable satisfaction, out ran the very first pressing of The Hurst's orchard. Bucket by bucket the macerated fruit went through the system, as our team laboured to bottle our abundant harvest. The final count was 100 bottles of fresh juice.

We made new friends on all sides – by a generous donation to the Scrumpers and most important, we passed over our final tray-load for transformation into cider for the village barrel. Invited to the Wassailing, we knew we had been accepted."

From The Hurst apple correspondent

Straddling the Shropshire Herefordshire border were hundreds of orchards. Many produced cider for the farm workers. Orchards were lost but strenuous efforts are being made to restore the neglected ones and to plant traditional varieties. Apples feature in many seasonal recipes.

Clive of India's Apple Chutney

At Edenbridge John and Helen weekly patronised the *Quality Tandoori Restaurant* on the High Street. John was guest of honour on the first night. "... we asked the local people who was a well-known person in the public eye and we were kindly recommended Mr John Osborne, the playwright."

Within ten miles of The Hurst are two estates purchased with Clive of India's great fortune - Walcot near Bishop's Castle and Oakly Park near Ludlow. In homage to the virtual founder of the empire in India, this chutney has a more authentic taste than the sweeter mass-produced ones.

At The Hurst this chutney home-made from the apples of the orchard is served. Writers have enjoyed it enough to take jars home. I prefer chutney which has retained the texture of its ingredients rather than a mush. You should be able to discern the individual cubes of apple. Bramleys are best though I have used the windfall apples at random and everyone still enthuses. The secret is the use of oil and frying the spices.

Makes about 3.2kg/7lb

2.5kg/5^1/$_2$lb apples [Bramleys would be best] peeled, cored, chopped into ^{1}/$_2$ inch cubes
10tbsp salt
7.5cm/3inch ginger, peeled
3 chopped fresh green chillies, with seeds removed
5 whole heads garlic, peeled
320ml/11fl oz sunflower oil
5tsp ground turmeric
3tbsp ground cumin
3tbsp fenugreek seeds
5tbsp black peppercorns
10tbsp mustard seeds
575g/1^1/$_4$lb dark brown sugar
750ml/25fl oz cider vinegar

Chop the apples, sprinkle with the salt. Allow to draw for an hour or more.

In a blender or processor make a paste of the garlic, ginger and chillies with just enough oil to prevent clogging [say 125ml/4fl oz].

If you have a large heavy-based pan you can begin making the chutney from the start but rather than have spices or the paste stick to the base you may prefer to make this phase in a frying pan. Heat the remaining 200ml/7fl oz oil on medium, add the peppercorns, fenugreek, and mustard seeds. The ground spices are less tolerant so hold them back until the first mustard seeds pop. Stir in the cumin and turmeric, remove from the heat. Add the paste from the garlic, ginger and chillies carefully to avoid spitting. Return to the heat and stir continuously for 7 or 8 minutes to avoid it catching. The paste will have taken on a cooked rather than raw appearance.

If using a frying pan, now is the time to transfer the ingredients to a large saucepan. Raise the heat to medium and add the apples and vinegar. Bring slowly to the boil before adding the sugar. Warming the sugar in the oven will assist rapid dissolving and avoid the risk of any sticking to the bottom of the pan. Simmer for up to 3 hours when the chutney will be an appealing dark brown.
When making up the chutney in sterilised jars leave a little space for topping off with some of the spiced oil.

Casserole of Pheasant with Juniper & Apple

What may be a semi-luxury in the supermarket is two-a-penny for the country dweller. A day out with a gun may cost a hundred pounds a bird but the imbalance of supply and demand means that birds 'in the feather' cost less than any other meat. As roadkill they're an even better bargain.

2 medium pheasants
225g/8oz streaky bacon chopped
2 tbsp juniper berries crushed
4 tbsp Calvados or brandy
225g/8oz shallots or pickling onions
2 sticks celery sliced
1 bay leaf
4 tbsp flour
Salt & pepper
1 bottle red wine
4 dessert apples
25/1oz butter

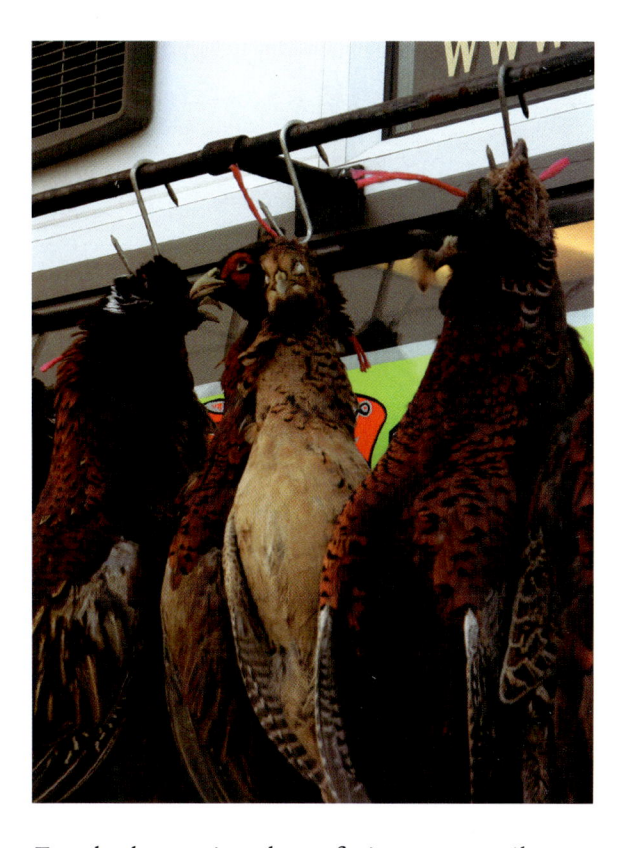

Fry the bacon in a large frying pan until crisp, remove and set aside. Toss the juniper berries into the same fat for one minute. Remove. Add the pheasants, cook and turn until all sides are brown.
Place the birds into a large oven-proof casserole and add the bacon and juniper berries.

In another pan warm the spirits, pour over the birds and ignite. Add the shallots, celery and bay leaf. Stir the flour and seasoning into the remaining fat in the frying pan and slowly add the wine to make a smooth sauce. Boil, then pour over the pheasants in the casserole.

Cover and cook in a moderate oven 180C, 350F, gas4 for $1^{1}/_{4}$ - $1^{1}/_{2}$ hours. Core the apples and slice into rings. In melted butter brown the apples in a frying pan. Drain and add to the casserole before serving.

Venison Steaks with Port and Rowan Jelly or Redcurrant Sauce

2 Venison steaks cut from the leg
2 large field mushrooms

2 tbsp port [or red wine]
2 tbsp red currant or rowan jelly

For the Rowan jelly recipe see page 67

Put a pat of butter in the centre of each steak and dust with pepper & salt. With the mushrooms beneath to catch the juices of the meat, grill the steaks.
Set aside the steaks and keep warm with the mushrooms. To the juices in the grill pan add the port or red wine and the rowan or red currant jelly. Scrape up the residue from the pan and mix well.

Red Cabbage

700g/1½lb cabbage
50g/2oz butter
50g/2oz soft brown sugar
4 tbsp red wine vinegar
1 tbsp red currant jelly

Remove the outer leaves and quarter the cabbage before shredding. Melt the butter in a heavy-bottomed saucepan, stir in the sugar and add the wine vinegar. Add the cabbage and stir. Cover and leave to cook over the lowest heat for two hours, stirring occasionally. Add the red currant jelly to the dish before serving.

Shropshire Fitchet Pie

First catch your polecat. Fitchett is a 17th century word for weasel or polecat.

This simple cottagers' dish made use of the pig from their sty and the windfalls. Now it is the subject of gentrification. National food group *Taste Real Food* organised a fidget pie competition in Ludlow. The Ludlow Food Centre, Bromfield has sold its 10,000th pie. In acquiring this posher accent, the pie uses gammon from Gloucester Old Spot pigs, "potatoes and apples grown on their Oakly Park estate, cheddar cheese made in their dairy and mustard made in their jam and pickle kitchen."

With John's preference for the plain and simple, I have turned back to Florence White's *Good Things in England* which quoted Mrs Dale's Fidget Pie an authentic Shropshire recipe. I have adapted the recipe.

225g/8oz shortcrust pastry
325g/12oz unsmoked bacon chopped
2 medium onions, chopped
450g/1lb Bramley apples, peeled and sliced
450g/1lb potatoes, peeled and sliced
300ml/ ½ pint strong chicken stock
Salt and pepper

If you prefer a tart dish then Bramleys hold their shape better than a sweeter apple. You may add sugar to sweeten the overall taste.

Place a layer of potatoes at the bottom of a deep pie dish. Alternate layers of onion, bacon and potato, and season each layer with salt and pepper finishing with bacon. Pour the chicken stock over.

Bake in a preheated oven at 170C/325F gas 4 for 40 minutes. Roll out a pastry lid for the top. Bake for a further 20 minutes at 190C/375F gas 6 until the pastry browns.

Damson Sauce - a topping for Ice Cream

The climate of The Marches is most suited to the damson – supposedly brought back from Damascus by the crusaders. The damson, like wimberies, was a vital cash crop for the smallholders in the Shropshire Hills. With the Shropshire Prune the county has its very own variety. Gnarled damson trees sprawl in many a hedgerow, garden and even the occasional orchard.

Individual growers still bring their harvests to the local markets for those keen to make damson gin, cheese and jam.

450g/1lb damsons
150ml/ ¼ pt water
110 – 175g/4 – 6 oz sugar
1 heaped tsp arrowroot
Stew the damsons with the water. Sieve through a strainer until you have a pulp. Return to the pan. Add sugar to taste. When dissolved blend arrowroot with a little juice in a cup. Gradually add to the sauce and blend until slightly thick. Omit the arrowroot if you prefer a thinner sauce.

Serve over ice cream.

Blackberry & Apple Dumplings

450g/1lb short crust pastry
4 large cooking apples preferably Bramleys
225g/8oz blackberries
4 tbsp soft brown sugar
1/2 tsp ground cinnamon
1/2 tsp ground cloves
Small quantity of whole milk

Peel and generously core the apples. Mix the spices with the sugar. Combine with the blackberries. Roll out 4 circles of pastry using a saucer as your guide. Place an apple in each. Fill the cores with the blackberry mixture. Heap the residue over the apples. Brush the edges of the pastry with milk, bring together to enrobe the fruit and seal.

Place on a greased baking tray. Brush over with the milk. Bake at 220C/400F, gas 6.

At Christmas this can be given a seasonal twist with mincemeat in place of the berries.

Bonfire Toffee Apples

If there's a secret with this simple dish, it's getting the right contrast between sharp and sweet. You'll need medium-sized apples with a certain tartness.

450g/1lb sugar
110g/4oz butter
2 tbsp water
12 apples approx
Lollipop sticks

Wash the apples and insert the sticks. Using a heavy saucepan over a low hear, dissolve the sugar and butter in the hot water. Slowly bring to the boil, stirring to avoid the syrup catching. Boil to the "small crack" 290F if you have a sweet making thermometer (otherwise drop a teaspoonful into ice cold water. Remove and see if it snaps with a small noise). Dip each apple into cold water and then into the toffee. Repeat the process and lay out on buttered parchment or greaseproof paper.

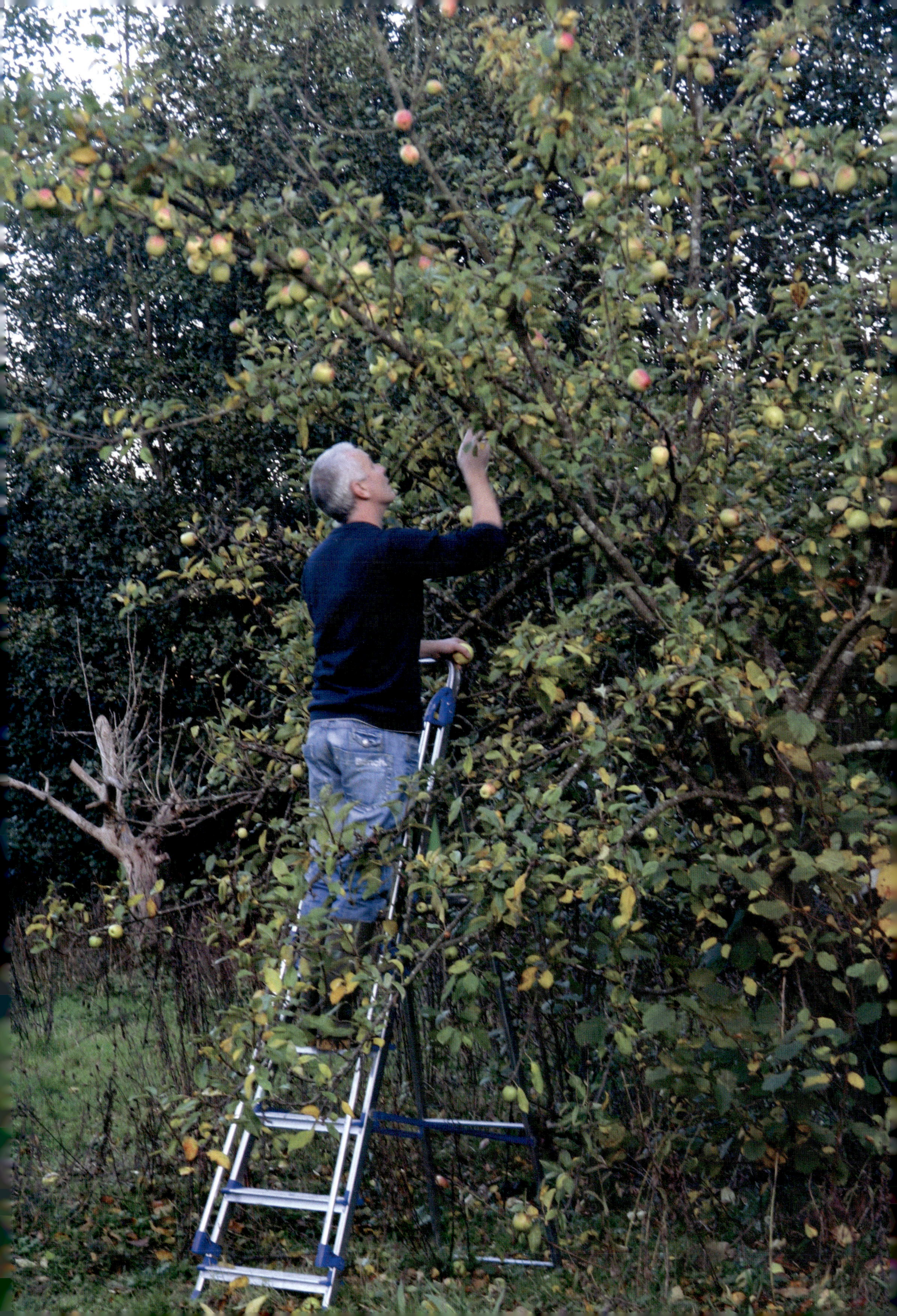

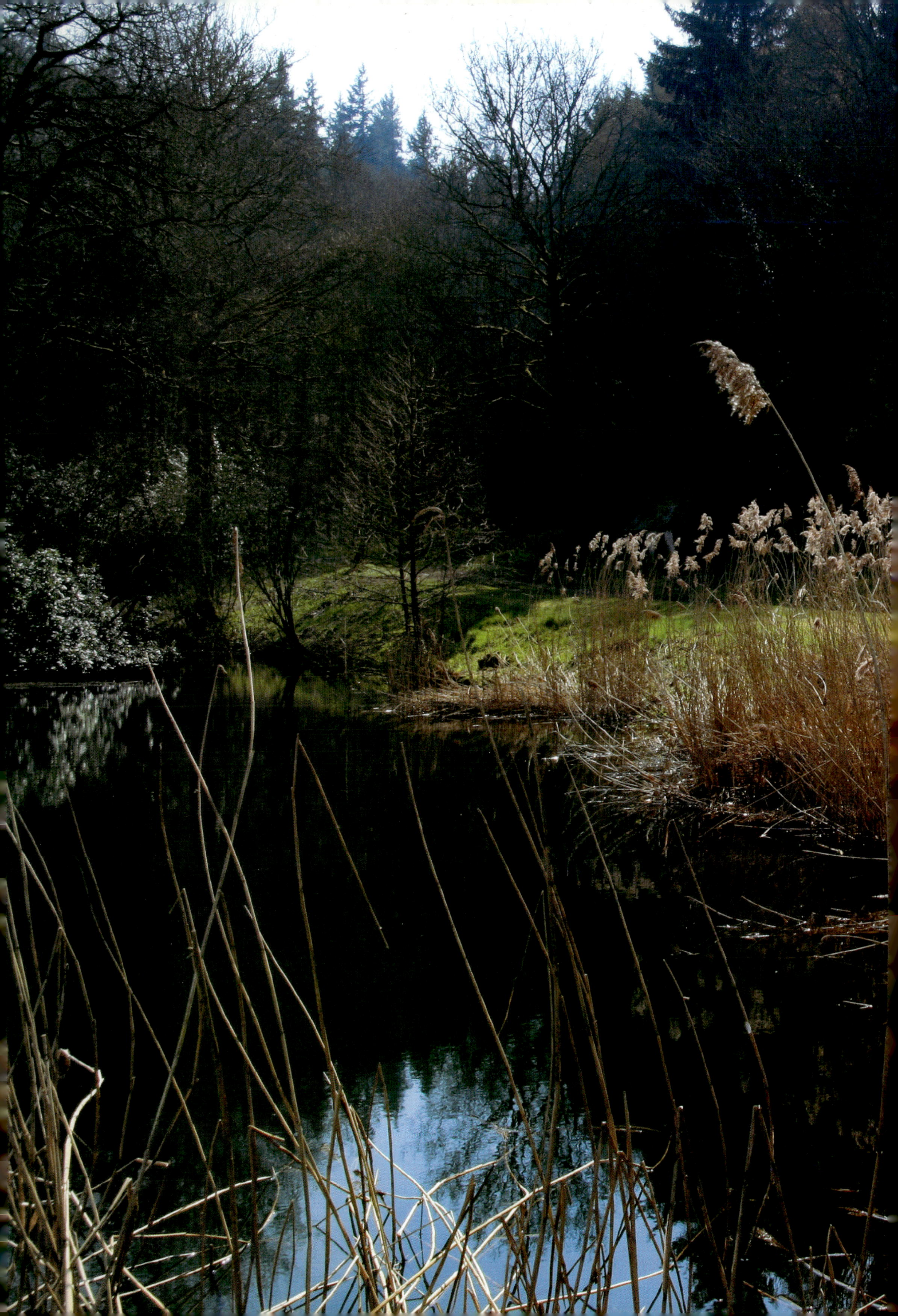

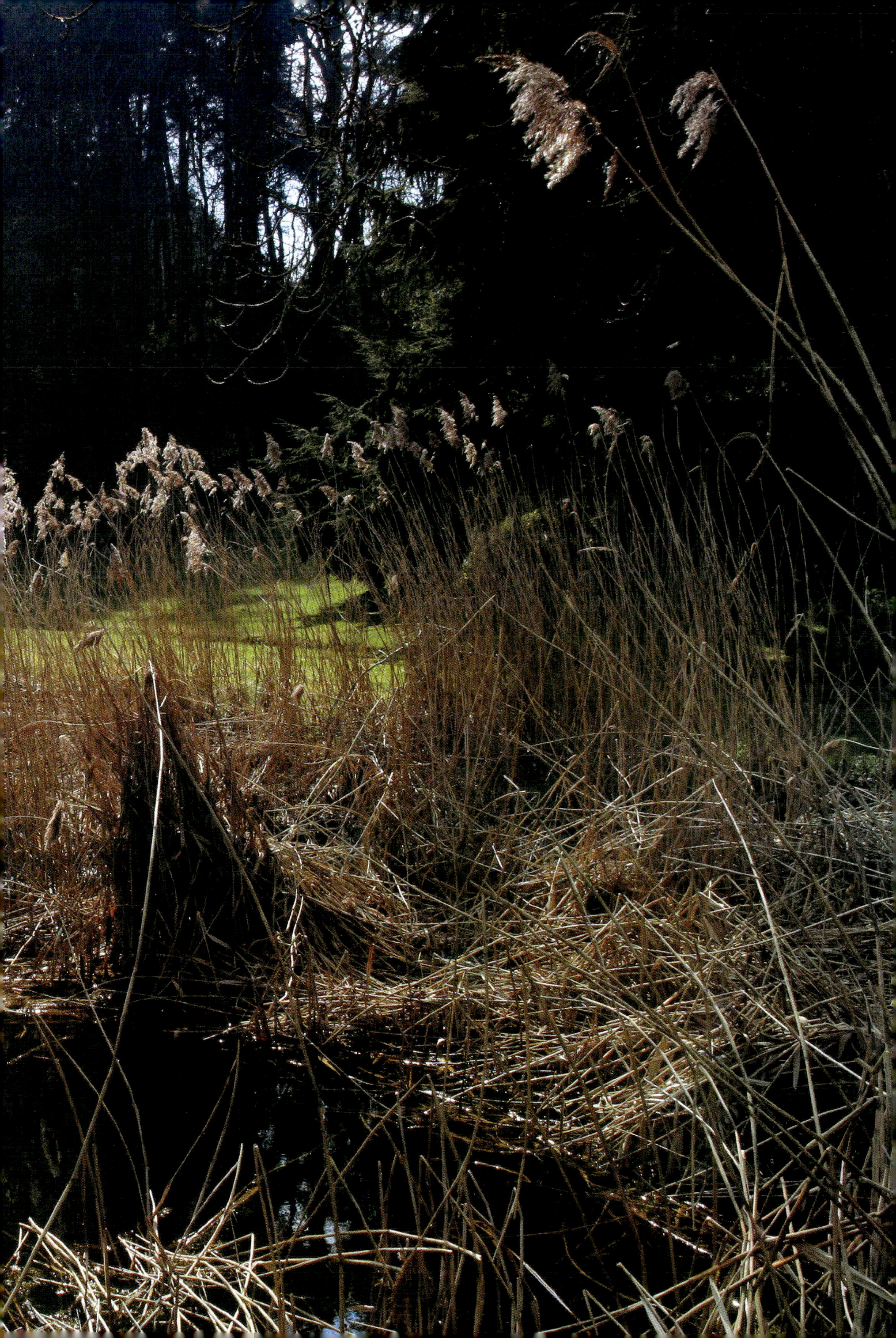

WINTER

Beef casserole in the orchard
Potato Latkes
Helen's fish cakes
Little orange custard pots
Wine jelly
Christmas ham

Beef Casserole in the Orchard

Serves 6

1kg/2.2lb stewing beef
2 tbsp cider vinegar
3 onions peeled and sliced
4 celery stalks sliced
200g/7oz chestnut mushrooms
50g/2oz butter
25g/1oz flour
750ml/2$^{1}/_{2}$pt dry cider
Salt & pepper

Ask butcher to cut beef into a dozen pieces.

Pre-heat the oven to 150C/300F/gas3.

Gently brown the meat on both sides in a frying pan with oil or dripping. Put the beef on one side and fry the onion, celery and mushrooms in butter in the same pan. Sprinkle on the flour and allow to brown all over, stir in the cider, bring to the boil.

Place the beef in an ovenproof casserole and add the vegetable/cider stock. Season. Cook in the oven until the meat is tender about 3 hours.

Helen's Fish Cakes

The 'DHSS' friends recall this was one of Helen's regular contributions to their meetings.

450g/1lb poached fish
450g/1lb cooked potato
Squeeze of lemon juice
grated zest of $^{1}/_{4}$ lemon
1 tbsp chopped parsley
Pinch of cayenne pepper
1 egg beaten
Breadcrumbs

Loosely mash the potatoes, then combine with the flaked fish and other ingredients. Form into small round cakes. Dip into beaten egg and breadcrumbs.

Helen's tip: to keep their shape place in the freezer or fridge for at least 30 minutes. Fry in oil until brown on both sides.

Serve with tartare sauce.

Potato Latkes

One of John's everyday favourite meals was pork sausages or garlic sausage which he liked accompanied by this traditional Jewish dish.

450g/1lb grated raw potato
1tbsp grated or very finely chopped onion
2 large eggs
2 tbsp flour
Salt & pepper

Peel and grate the potatoes into a mixing bowl, combine with the onions and flour, stir in well-beaten eggs. The mixture should be soft enough to drop from the spoon. Add another egg if too thick.

Heat some oil in a frying pan, when hot drop in spoonfuls of the mixture and fry until brown on both sides.

Little Orange Custard Pots

When John and Helen arrived at The Hurst, Caroline Denham and Martin Poole had already established a reputation for good food. The Old Post Office, Clun had won a star rating in *The Budget Good Food Guide*.

Serves 6

6 egg yolks
3 egg whites
5 tbsp caster sugar
Vanilla pod
750ml/1¼ pts milk
Grated rind and juice of 1 orange
2 tbsp Cointreau
Unsalted butter

Beat the egg yolks and whites together with 2 tbsp of the sugar. Heat the milk freshly grated orange rind, vanilla pod and the rest of the sugar without letting it boil. Remove the vanilla pod. Pour the milk mixture over the eggs, whisking all the time. Whisk in the

Cointreau and the orange juice. Strain the mixture into well-buttered ramekins.

Place the ramekins in a pan of hot water and bake at 190C, 375F gas 5, for about 1 hour until the custards are set. Sprinkle the top with raw cane sugar while still warm.

They can be eaten hot or cold and if you really feel like spoiling yourself, instead of sprinkling sugar on top, make an orange/Cointreau syrup, or for a sharper taste an orange/Calvados syrup; turn out the custards and pour the syrup over the top.

Karen Wallace Shropshire Food 1986

Wine Jelly

Serves 6

Wine jelly was a popular pudding in the 18th and 19th centuries. Diane Davis's recipe is especially good after a large, rich meal.

1 wetted jelly mould or 6 Champagne flutes
300ml/ ½pt dry sherry
4 tbsp orange juice
3 tbsp lemon juice
150g/6oz sugar dissolved in 450ml/ ¾pt boiling water
Gelatine

Measure the liquid, including the sugar and place in a bowl. For every pint of liquid dissolve 15g/½ oz or 1 sachet of gelatine in 2 tbsp of water in a saucepan. Do not boil. Stir into the rest of the liquid and pour into a mould or glasses and allow to set.

Karen Wallace Shropshire Food 1986

Christmas Ham

The Clun butcher, Frank Wells, would supply this joint for an attractive Boxing Day buffet dish. Everyone has a favourite glaze.

1.8kg/4lb piece of gammon
Cloves
175g/ 6oz black treacle
A little beer

Soak the ham overnight in cold water – at least 8 hours. Weigh and place in a large pan on an inverted saucer or a trivet. Cover the ham with cold water. Bring to a boil and reduce to simmer for 45minutes per kilo/ 20 minutes per lb. Ensure the ham is covered by the liquid, topping up if required.

Pre-heat the oven to 190C, 375F, gas 5. Remove the gammon from the saucepan and wipe dry. Remove the skin. Score the surface into diamonds. Combine the black treacle with the beer and spread over the surface of the meat. Stud the diamonds with the cloves.

I have found glazes can be very sensitive – you should keep an eye on its progress. It will take from at least 15 minutes to perhaps 30 minutes.

Alternative glaze: combine 175g/6oz marmalade with the zest and juice of two oranges, brush over the ham.

Garnish with apples or tropical fruit.

John, ever the traditionalist, loved his mince pies. His favourite were those made by Sue Dowell. If you fancy taking your taste buds on a journey through time, stop at the 18th century when the **minced-meat** pie still included meat. I first encountered this version in Pézenas where they bake around 150,000 a year of their 'petits pâtés' following a recipe they had from Clive of India in 1768. The combination of meat, fruit, sugar and spices may sound unusual but it goes back to our great medieval pies.

I have a leather-bound manuscript cookbook 1842 from Dothill Park, Wellington which contains a recipe which includes tongue, rendered and pounded suet … I'm no lover of tongue, but with the addition of "2 wine glasses of port, half a pint of sherry and half that quantity of brandy … add a little more brandy when made into pies" even this strange meat would slip down.

Mince Pies.

One pound & half of baked Tongue pounded. 3lbs of suet rendered, & pounded. 3lbs of Apples grated 3lbs of Currants nicely washed. 2lbs of Raisins stoned and chopt a little. 3lbs of good moist Sugar, and the rind and juice of 3 Lemons, quarter of an Ounce of Mace the same of Cinnamon, half a quater of an Ounce of Nutmegs, the same of Cloves, 2 wineglasses of Port half a pint of Sherry & half that quantity of Brandy Mix well together, put down in a Jar closely covered & kept in a dry place. Add Candied peel, & a little more brandy when made into pies.

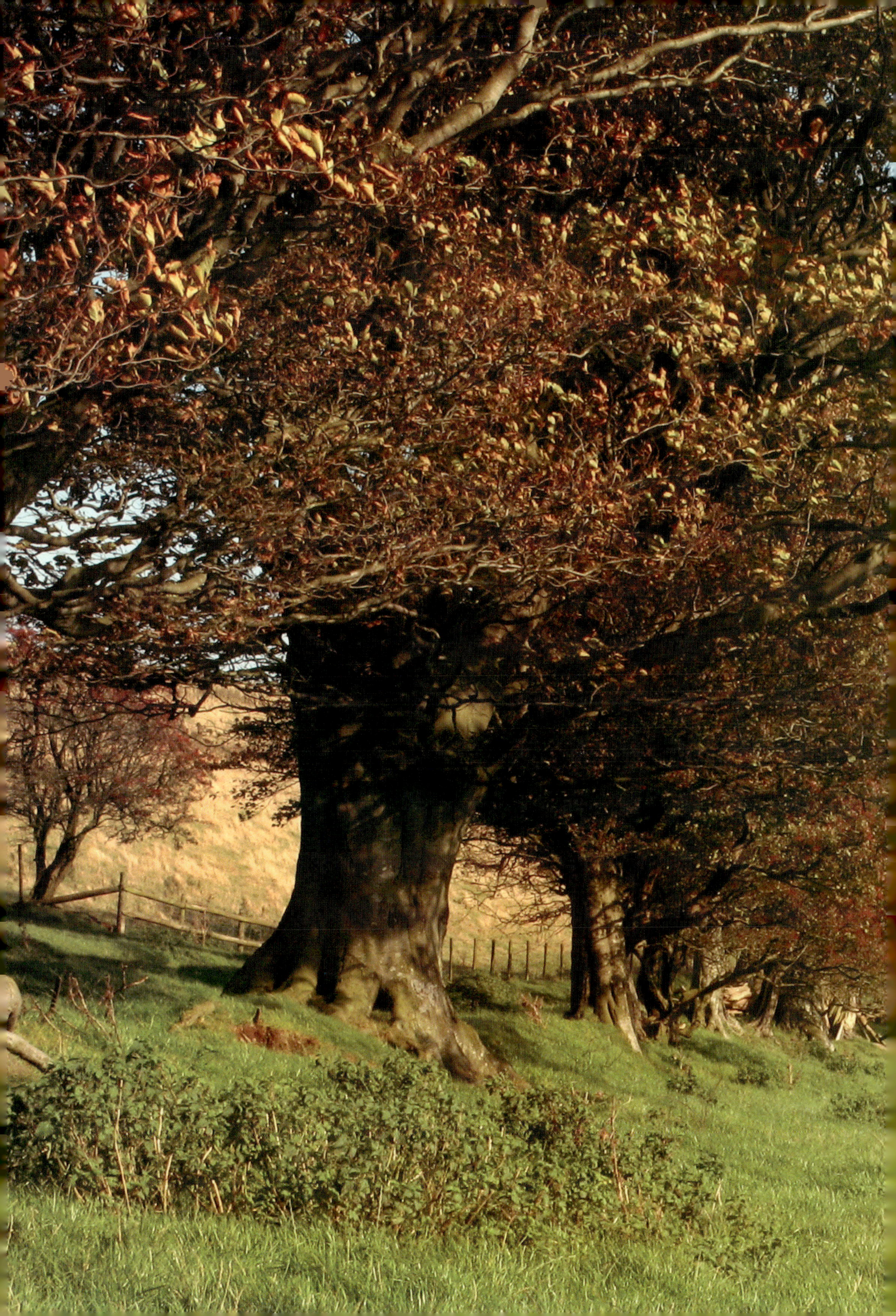

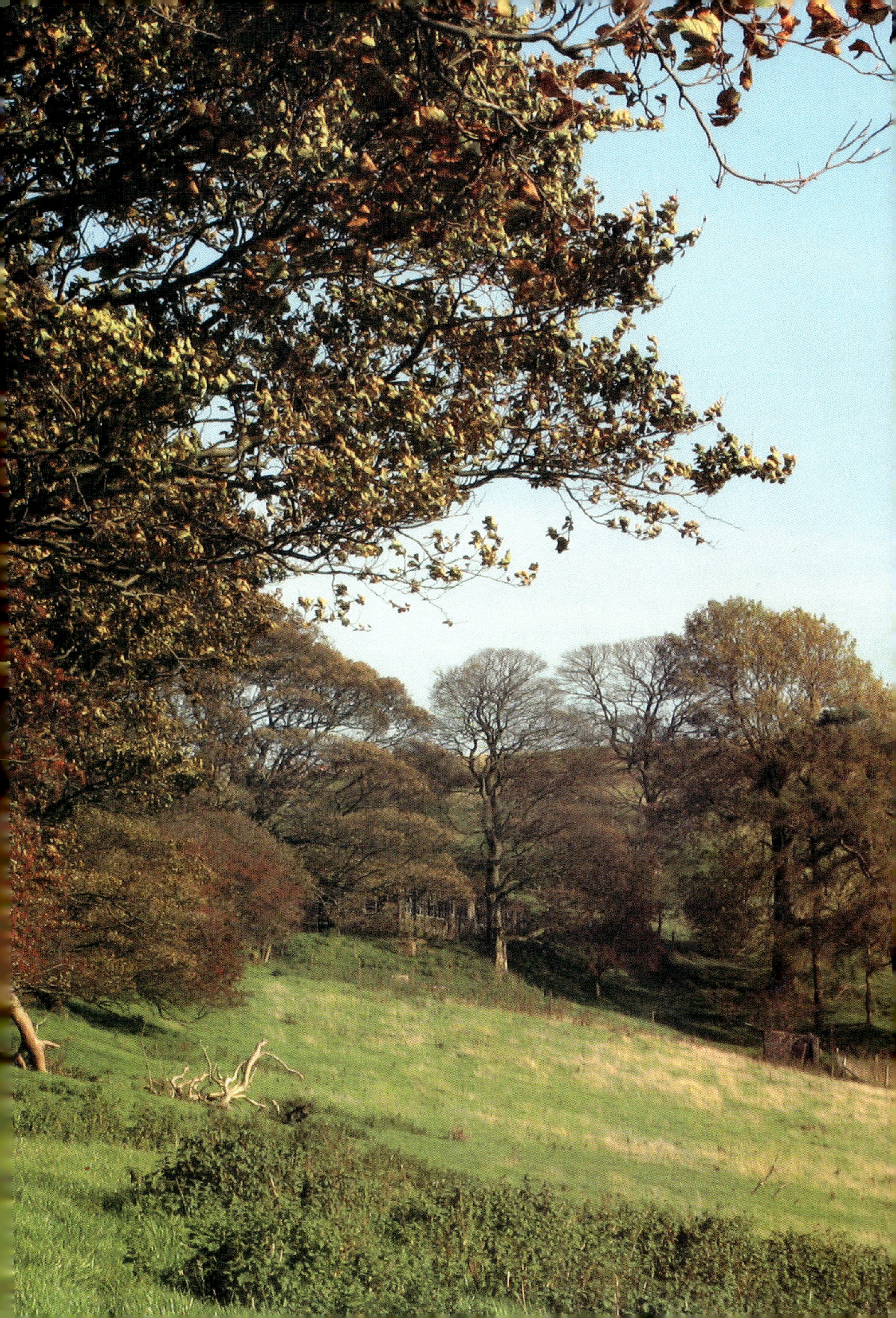

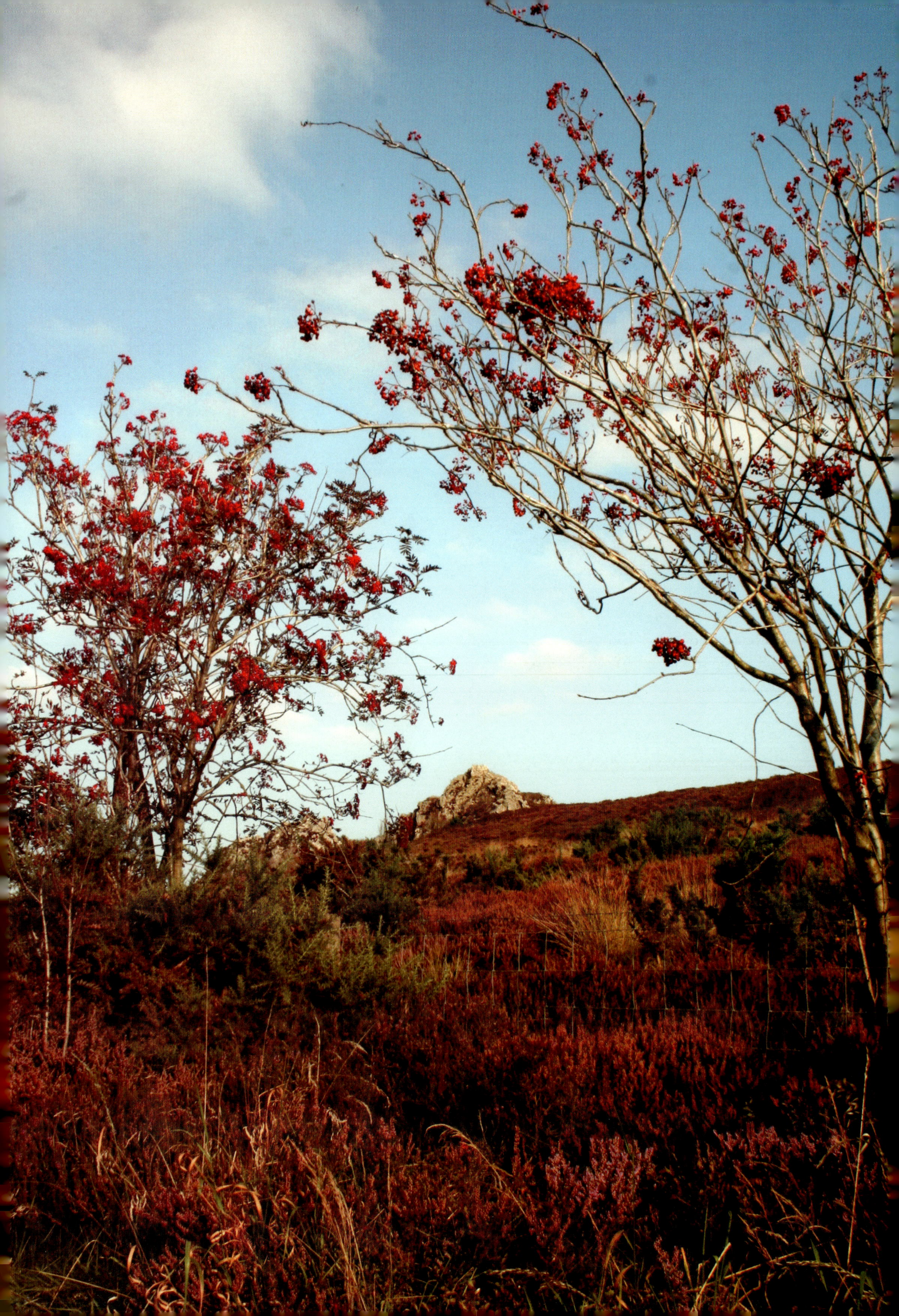

THE WILD THINGS

Shropshire, a vast rural county, is a treasure store of wild food. For Helen and John their first walk, the first Spring in the surrounding wilderness would have been a joy.
In past days foraging for wild food was a necessity for the poor, but today it has become as fashionable as designer clothes. Recommended by chefs, it has to be trendy.

Forget the old colander and crock basin, a plastic bag to gather blackberries or elderflowers. Eyes down, green-wellied, swinging a special mushroom basket, the simple pleasures are back. Truffles they may not be, but the sight and smell of newly picked mushrooms or puffballs is a rare treat.

No one could resist picking the scent-laden wild garlic [ramsons] from the banks of the stream through The Hurst Dingle.

As the seasons flowed – so the variety of wild things gathered pace, complementing the menus of yesterday and today.

Nettle and wild garlic soup
St George's mushrooms and chicken livers
Elderflower Cheesecake
Elderflower Cordial
Wimberry Clafoutis
Kerry's wild strawberry jam
Rowan Jelly
Fried Puff balls
Hedgerow Jelly – Ruth Mapes
Hazelnut brownies
Sloe Gin

Nettle and Wild Garlic Soup

John Osborne and his actor friend Anthony Creighton lived on the Motor Yacht Egret moored on the Thames. The banks of the river which yielded a fine crop of nettles made up for the absence of any restaurants.

Serves 4

110g/4oz young nettles
110g/4oz wild garlic leaves
1 onion chopped
1 medium potato peeled and chopped
25g/1oz butter
1litre /2 pts vegetable stock
1 tsp ground coriander
Pinch chilli powder [optional]

I have matched the quantities to fit in the

largest saucepan of an average household providing enough space for the large volume of nettles and wild garlic leaves.

225g /1/2lb young nettles
225g/ 1/2lb wild garlic leaves if you can find them
2 onions
1 medium potato peeled and chopped
25g/1oz butter
2 pints vegetable stock
2 tsp ground coriander
Pinch chilli powder optional

First don your rubber gloves. With scissors cut the young shoots of the nettles.
Wash the nettles and wild garlic leaves. Chop the wild garlic.

Chop the onions and fry gentle in the butter until soft. Add the coriander and pinch of chilli. Blend in. Add the stock and peeled, chopped potato. Boil and simmer until the potato is soft. Add the nettles and wild garlic leaves. In a few minutes they will shrink. Remove the pot from the stove and liquidise into a bright green soup.
I had this recipe in 1985 from Arthur Hollins of Ford Hall Farm, Market Drayton a pioneer of organic farming. He was no softie, brave enough without gloves to drag the leaves from below. The Hurst has such a fine crop of wild garlic along The Dingle from early March to May that I have added them to Arthur's original recipe.

The Shropshire Hills Area of Outstanding Natural Beauty has over 600 miles of brooks, streams and rivers. Nowhere are you more than half a mile from flowing water. Wild garlic loves damp, shady conditions, in season you should have no difficulty in locating them following your nose.

St George's Mushrooms and Chicken Livers

Serves 4 as a starter

Even if these unique spring mushrooms don't always appear in time for April 23rd – St George's Day, Shakespeare's birthday – they are worth waiting for.

Is this a very old joke at the expense of our Norman conquerors? In French they are called mousserons, which we adopted as mushroom. St George's was perhaps a bit of national defiance.

Titterstone Clee is like a geological layer cake. For once you should head not for the summit but for the lower layers where old limestone workings provide the ideal nursery for this creamy white fungus. The time of year will help with identification but as a further guide use your nose, when picked they give off a powerful yeasty smell. They also flourish in parts of the Long Mynd, but my husband fears competition in his favourite location.

St George's mushrooms are traditionally picked and eaten on St George's day, 23 April. They look rather like pure-white field mushrooms and have a similar meaty flavour. Keen foragers could throw some wild garlic leaves in with the mushrooms and livers at the end.

225g/8oz fresh chicken livers
2-3tbsp olive oil
225g/8oz St George's mushrooms halved or quartered if large
2 cloves of garlic,
Salt and freshly ground black pepper
60g/2½oz butter
1tbsp chopped parsley

Pat the livers dry and season with salt & pepper.

Peel and crush the garlic with the blade of a knife. Heat olive oil in a heavy-based frying pan and quickly fry the livers for a minute on each side, until still pink inside. Reserving the livers on one side, clean the pan and heat a little olive oil.

Add the mushrooms, garlic, season with salt

and pepper and fry over a high heat for a few minutes, stirring occasionally, until they begin to soften and are lightly coloured. Return the livers to the pan with the mushrooms and add the butter. Cook for another minute and add the parsley. Stir well and spoon on to warmed serving plates.

Elderflower Cheesecake

In June and July the lanes of the Shropshire Hills are lined with the creamy white sprays of elderflower. Here's a recipe which has its roots in medieval England. It is important to use the flowers as soon as possible after picking – leaving them overnight is not a good idea.

The works of Mary Webb celebrate the rich harvest of the Shropshire Hills. It takes a brave man to serve her loyal disciples with a feast in her honour. Yet Simon Smith, the Shropshire Chef, rose to the challenge when the Mary Webb Society came to The Hurst for their summer school in 2008. Gordon Dickins, Chairman of the Society, enjoyed the dish so much, now he cannot wait for the first elderflowers to appear.

225g/8oz rich shortcrust pastry
4 eggs, separated
110g/4oz caster sugar
350g/12oz cream cheese
75g/3oz fresh breadcrumbs
3-4 sprigs of fresh elderflowers or 1 tbsp elderflower cordial
2-3 fresh edible flowers, for decoration

Pre-heat the oven to 180°C/350F/gas 4
Line a deep 23cm/9in tart tin with the pastry and pre-bake or bake blind for about 10-15 minutes.
In a bowl, cream together the egg yolks and sugar until almost white and shiny, then gradually add the cream cheese, beating well after each addition until well blended. Stir in the breadcrumbs and set aside.
Prepare the freshly picked elderflowers by forking the flowers off the stems. Stir the flowers or cordial into the cheese mixture.
In a separate bowl, whisk the egg whites until shiny and stiff, then fold these into the cheesy mixture. Spoon into the pre-baked pastry case. Bake in the oven for about 45 minutes or until golden brown.
Serve warm or at room temperature with cream or crème fraîche

Elderflower Cordial

20 heads of elderflower
1.8kg/4lb granulated or caster sugar
1.2l/2pts water
2 unwaxed lemons
75g/3oz citric acid

Shake the elderflowers to dislodge any insects, and then place in a large bowl. Grate the lemons and slice the fruit.

Put the sugar into a pan with the water and bring up to the boil, stirring until the sugar has completely dissolved.

Add the grated lemon, lemon slices, citric acid and the flowerheads.

Cover with a cloth and then leave at room temperature, stirring occasionally, for twenty four hours.

Next day, strain the cordial through muslin (or a new j-cloth rinsed out in boiling water), and pour into thoroughly cleaned glass or plastic bottles. Screw on the lids and pop into the cupboard ready to use.

To serve: dilute the elderflower cordial to taste with fizzy water, and serve over ice with a slice or two of lemon, or a sprig of mint floating on top.

Wimberry Clafoutis

"Of all wild fruits the wimberry, or cloud-berry, should rank first. Its colour is the bloomy purple of distant hills. It tastes of Faery. It will grow only in beautiful and mysterious places. High on the airy hill, far from any sound of village or hamlet, voice or bell--except the voice of the shepherd and the sheepbell's silver tinkle--is the chosen haunt of the wimberry. Countless acres are covered with the neat, shining bushes, tall beside the streams, lowly on the summits. In spring, the leaf green is splashed with a beautiful red, like the colour of a ladybird; then come pink flowers, honeyed and waxen, and above their sweet acres the large, almost black bumble-bees of the hills coast to and fro with their deep murmur, like far-off seas in a dream. At the end of June, when young curlews run among the bushes, like yellow chickens pencilled with brown, the fruit begins to ripen, but it is not often ready for picking until after Saint Swithun's [July 15th]. From that date until late September a tide of life, gipsy and cottager and dweller in the plain, flows up into our hills. To the Stiperstones, to the Longmynd, to the wild, lonely stretches of Clun Forest, come the stooping, neutral-tinted figures--the lads with their little home-made trucks, the wise babies whose wimberry-picking is not yet, and whose task is simply to be good. Alone beside the family kettle amid the day's provisions he sits, the baby, smiling, gazing trustfully at the blue, arching sky, so deeply saturated with wimberry juice that one doubts if many Saturday tubs will clean him. He achieves the end and aim of his day: he is good. On every side of him stretch the purple plateaux, dotted with busy figures. Here and there, at a lost signpost or a mountain ash, is the trysting-place of the wimberry higgler. Twice a week he appears with his cart and his rough pony, and over the green, deeply rutted tracks, down valleys brimful of shadow and along precipitous roads, the wimberries go on their journey to the cities of England".

Mary Webb
Spring of joy: nature essays Fruits of the earth

"[in Shrewsbury] The berries were brought in hampers that needed two men to lift them, and the purple juices dripped from them as from a wine vat."

Mary Webb *Golden Arrow*

450g/1lb wimberries
110g/4ozs caster sugar
55g/2ozs unsalted butter

Batter
3 large eggs
55g/2ozs caster sugar
120ml/4 fl.ozs milk [or crème fraîche for a richer batter]
110g/4ozs plain flour

Pre-heat oven to 200C/400F/gas6
Butter and sugar a ceramic baking dish
Melt butter in a saucepan over a low heat, put aside. Mix fruit and sugar in the dish.

Make the batter by beating the eggs and sugar in a mixer. Slowly add the milk or crème fraîche and flour. Add the melted butter. Pour batter over the wimberries
Bake 30 minutes until firm and golden.

Wimberries, being wild, have a unique intensity of taste. The imported blueberry is more watery but a still acceptable substitute.

John and Jean Gethin of Longmeadow End, Craven Arms reminded me of my days picking blåbär in Sweden. Even using a peigne [comb with long teeth] to draw through the low bushes it is a painstaking job. Yet together they were able sometimes to pick 100lbs in a day. Even then the crop is not ready to sell. Your harvest is full of tiny leaves and twigs. The Gethins use an old Hoover in blow mode to remove the debris. And still they go over the fruit once more with a pair of tweezers.

Wimberries have a long history of being an essential cash crop to the locals. Brian Griffin picked hundreds of pounds to pay for a pram. Schools closed to allow the children to help their parents. Frank Wells' wife, Winifred Vaughan, recalled picking them with her sister, Marjorie, on the Black Hill.

She said children were a special asset as they were 'nearer to the ground'. Other parents have told me you had to ensure the young folk didn't include any sheep droppings.

On the Long Mynd you will find plenty of competition from sheep and other pickers. Serious pickers have their favourite out-of-the-way spots. I have found wimberries galore on The Stiperstones as late as end September. Both the Stiperstones Inn and the Bog Centre have wimberry specialities. At the Inn it's the delicious crumble and at the Bog Centre wimberry tart.

Kerry's Wild Strawberry Jam

If the wimberry can be a tiresome fruit to pick, the wild strawberry is even more perverse. The berries are masters of concealment, hiding under the leaves. They are even closer to the ground making this a back-breaking search.

Kerry Watson of The Hurst had tracked down just enough of the elusive berries to make a tiny pot of jam for tea. From the kitchen she appeared bearing the shining offering. The jam was proof that the wild berry amply makes up in concentrated sweetness for its size. It was delicious.

450g/1lb wild strawberries
350g/12oz preserving sugar

Soak the berries in half the sugar overnight. Strain off the juice and boil with the remainder of the sugar. Reduce slightly. Add the fruit and simmer for 20 minutes.
Pot into sterilised jars.
No amount of boiling will thicken wild strawberry like other jams. Their fragrance is so delicate and precious that the less boiling the better the final product.

Rowan Berry Jelly

In 2009 we had the best year for rowan berries I can recall. At the foot of Black Rhadley Hill the road from Bridges to Nind and the A488 meets the lane from Linley. From this remote crossroads to The Bog Centre is a spectacular display of scarlet berries. The whole area supports some of the finest rowans in England, especially Brook Vessons the Shropshire Wildlife Trust reserve on the northern slopes of The Stiperstones. The county claims the broadest rowan in the UK within 100 metres of the largest birch, the largest holly and the largest crab apple in Shropshire, not to mention several other rowan trees in the Top Ten.

You have a difficult choice to make. The berries will ripen from August to October but you may have to compete with the birds, so don't leave it too late.

Makes: 1.4 - 1.8kg /3 - 4lb

900g/2lb Rowan berries
900g /2lb Crab apples
1.8lt /3pts water
Sugar

Pick over the rowan berries, removing any stalks, wash if necessary, drying well.
Wash the whole crab apples, removing any bruised parts.
Place the fruit and just enough water to cover into a heavy bottomed saucepan. Bring to the boil and simmer, covered for 20 - 25 minutes, until tender.

Strain overnight through a jelly bag or muslin cloth, resist the temptation to squeeze the bag the jelly will become cloudy. Rowan Jelly has great eye-appeal and it should look jewel-like when the sun shines in your jars.

Measure the volume of the liquid; add 450g/1lb of sugar for each 600ml/1pint of liquid. Warm the sugar in the centre of a pre-heated oven for 10 - 15 minutes. This will help it dissolve more readily and reduce the risk of the sugar sticking to the bottom of the pan. Place the juice back into a heavy bottomed saucepan; add the sugar, stirring until fully dissolved.

Bring to the boil and cook rapidly for 10 - 15 minutes until the setting point is reached. Skim the surface if necessary; allow to cool slightly before adding to your jars.

Fried Puffballs

Colin and Ruth Mapes of Clun are keen mushroom foragers. They dry their chanterelles and ceps over the AGA. Their prize find was a cep weighing over 2 kilos.

Puffballs can grow to giant size before exploding. However, size isn't everything. As the puffballs mature, they first turn yellow and then brown.

1 large puffball
Rashers of streaky bacon or homecure bacon with plenty of fat

Clean and slice the puffball into 1cm/ $^1/_2$in steaks. Start with a small amount of oil just enough to grease the pan. Begin frying the bacon to release enough fat to cook the puffball steaks.

This is the essence of foraged meals – simplicity itself and yet very tasty.

Hazelnut Brownies

Many of the paths from the hamlets and villages leading up to the former commons of the Shropshire Hills are lined with hazels. Our forebears had to make their hedgerows as productive as possible. They could combine coppiced hazels for hurdles with a

The Wild Things

fine crop of nuts - especially as they didn't have to compete with the grey squirrel.

110g/4oz unsalted butter
75g/3oz hazelnut oil
275g/10oz dark chocolate, chopped
275g/10oz light soft brown sugar
3 medium eggs
55ml/2fl oz strong black coffee
110g/4oz rye flour
110g/4oz plain flour
½ tsp baking powder
150g/5oz toasted hazelnuts, skinned and roughly chopped

Melt the butter in a large saucepan, before adding the chocolate and oil, and stir over a low heat until melted. Beat in the sugar and eggs, then the coffee. Beat in the plain and rye flours and baking powder until smooth, and then stir in the nuts. Line a deep, 20cm-25cm/8in – 10in square cake tin with buttered greaseproof paper or baking parchment. Spoon in the mixture and smooth. Bake at 180C/350F/gas 4 for 30 minutes.

The best brownies are slightly squidgy.

Check five minutes before the end with a skewer just in case the oven cooks too quickly - if it comes out with a little of the mixture still adhering then it's done. The brownies will firm as they cool.

Remove from the oven and leave until the brownie is cold before cutting into squares.

Sloe Gin

Sloes, the fruit of the blackthorn, may be the sourest fruit you have ever tasted, but they make a wonderful drink, drier and more subtle than damson gin. With the years my palate may be growing more sophisticated but I am beginning to appreciate using the more up-market gins like Bombay Sapphire or Plymouth.

Sloe-pickers are best equipped with a stout pair of gloves to avoid martyrdom on the long spiky thorns. Unlike the rowans you need not fear competition from the birds. Wait until the first frost.

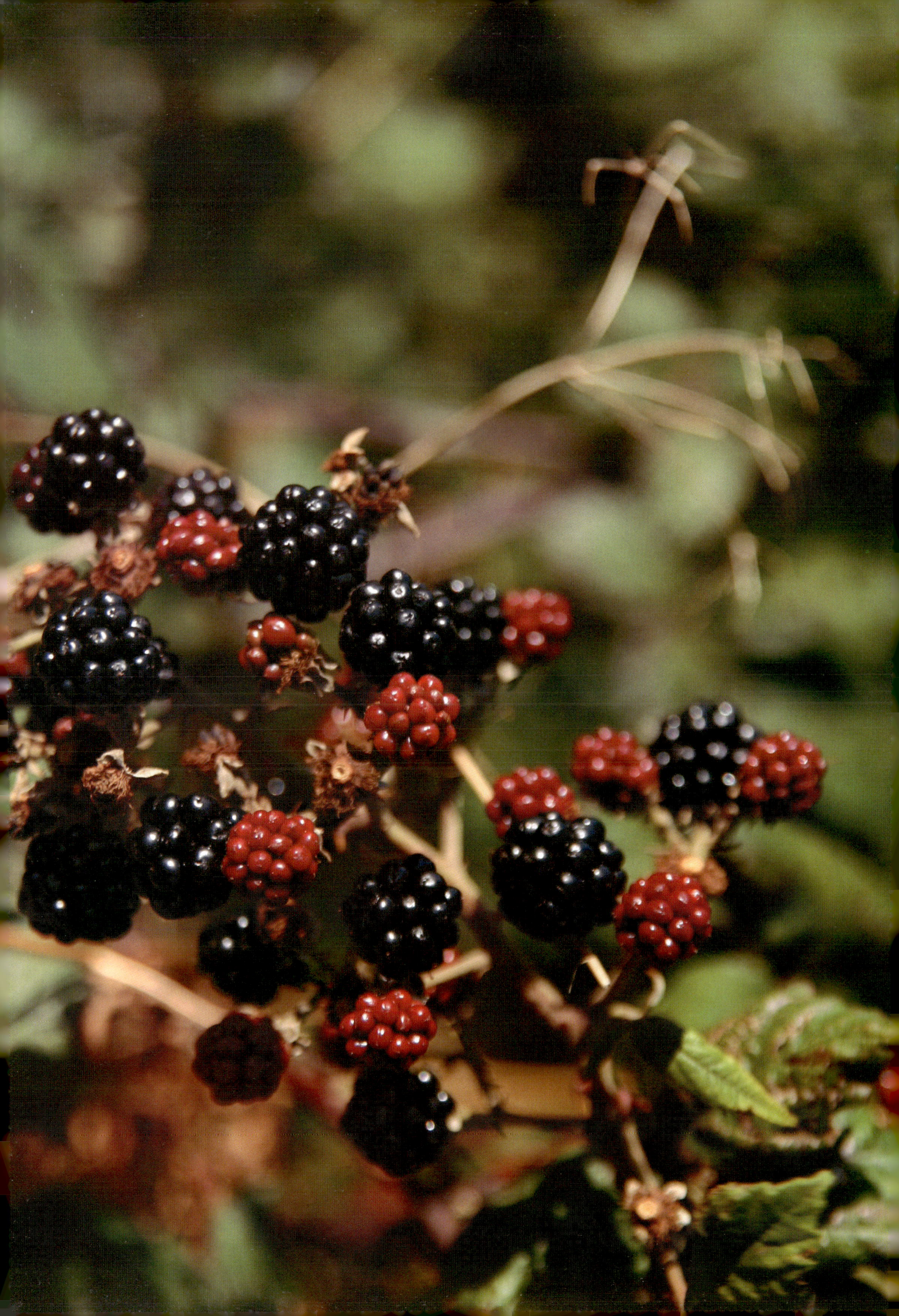

When you have gathered your harvest, put them in the freezer. This has the same effect as the labour-intensive task of pricking them with a thin skewer.

About 450g/1lb sloes
225g/ 8oz sugar
1 75cl bottle gin

Mix sloes with half the sugar. Layer the fruit and sugar in a jar. Add the gin [usually the whole bottle] to top up the jar. Close the jar and leave for about 2 months or longer, shaking occasionally. I aim to have ours ready for Christmas.

Hedgerow Jelly

Makes 5 to 6 jars

1kg/2.2lb crab apples [or Bramleys]
250g/9oz blackberries
250g/9oz damsons or bullaces
110g/4oz rose hips
110g/4oz wild cherries
110g/4oz elderberries
About 2l/3.5pts water
Up to 2kg/4.4lb sugar

Rinse and halve the crab apples [or cut up the Bramleys]. Remove stalks from the fruits and rinse. Place all fruits in a preserving pan. Add enough water to cover.

Boil and simmer until fruit is soft. Strain the juice through a jelly bag. Do not press it through, the juice should be clear.

Measure the juice before returning to the pan. For every 500ml/17fl oz of juice add 500g/1lb2oz of sugar. Stir over a low heat until the sugar dissolves.

Bring to the boil. Skim off any white foam. Lower the heat and simmer until setting pint is reached. Test: by putting a little of the jelly on to a cold saucer, leave to cool a little, push with the finger until it wrinkles. Pot in sterilised jars.

When cool, cover with rounds of greaseproof paper and seal.

Appropriately Ruth Mapes of Clun, vicar's daughter from More near Bishop's Castle, remembers her mother's belief in the fruits of the hedgerow as 'something for nothing.' Ruth now puts this to charitable use in creating her Hedgerow Jelly for the Joliba Trust – which supports grassroots development work with farming and cattle-raising communities in Mali. 'Joliba' is the local name for the River Niger, and means 'riches of life'.

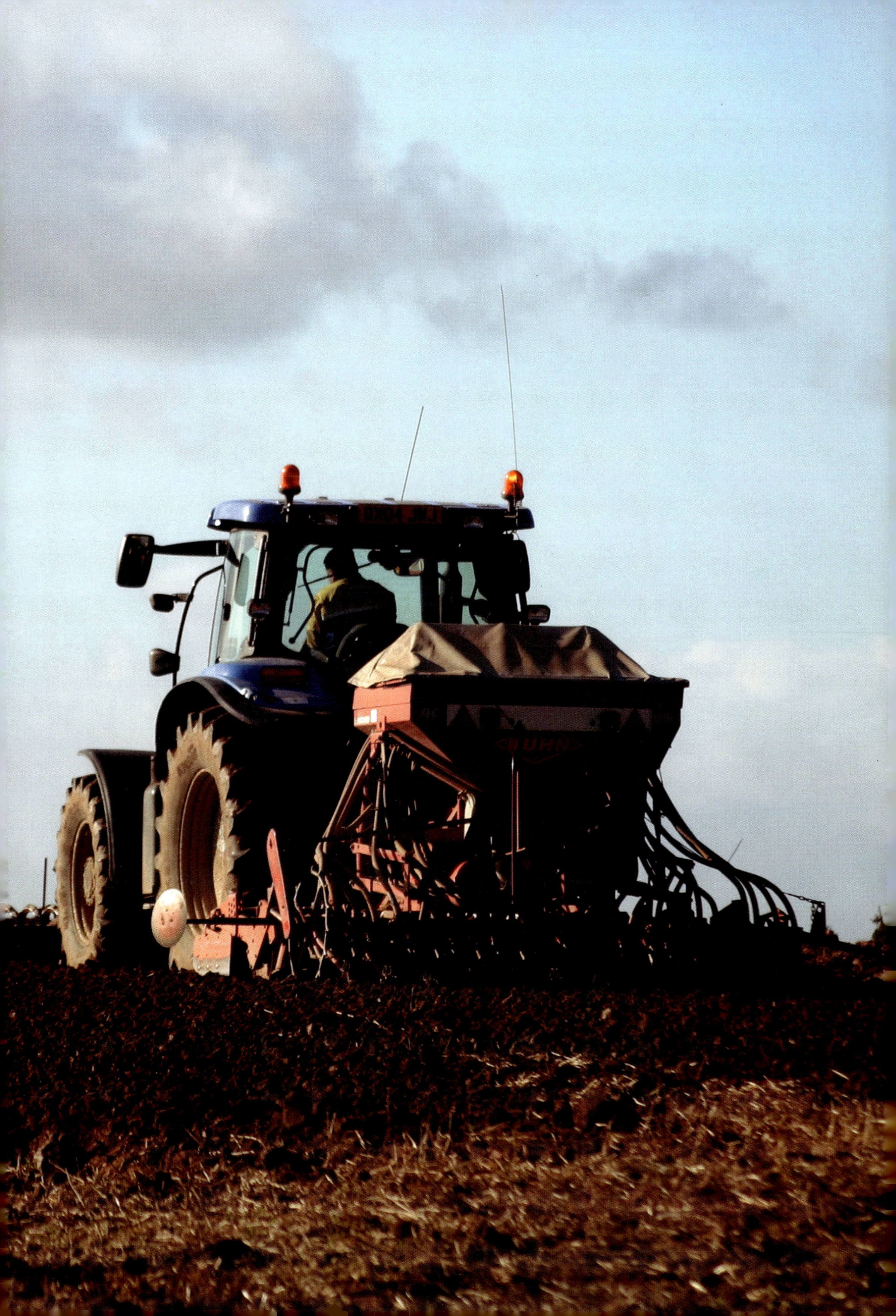

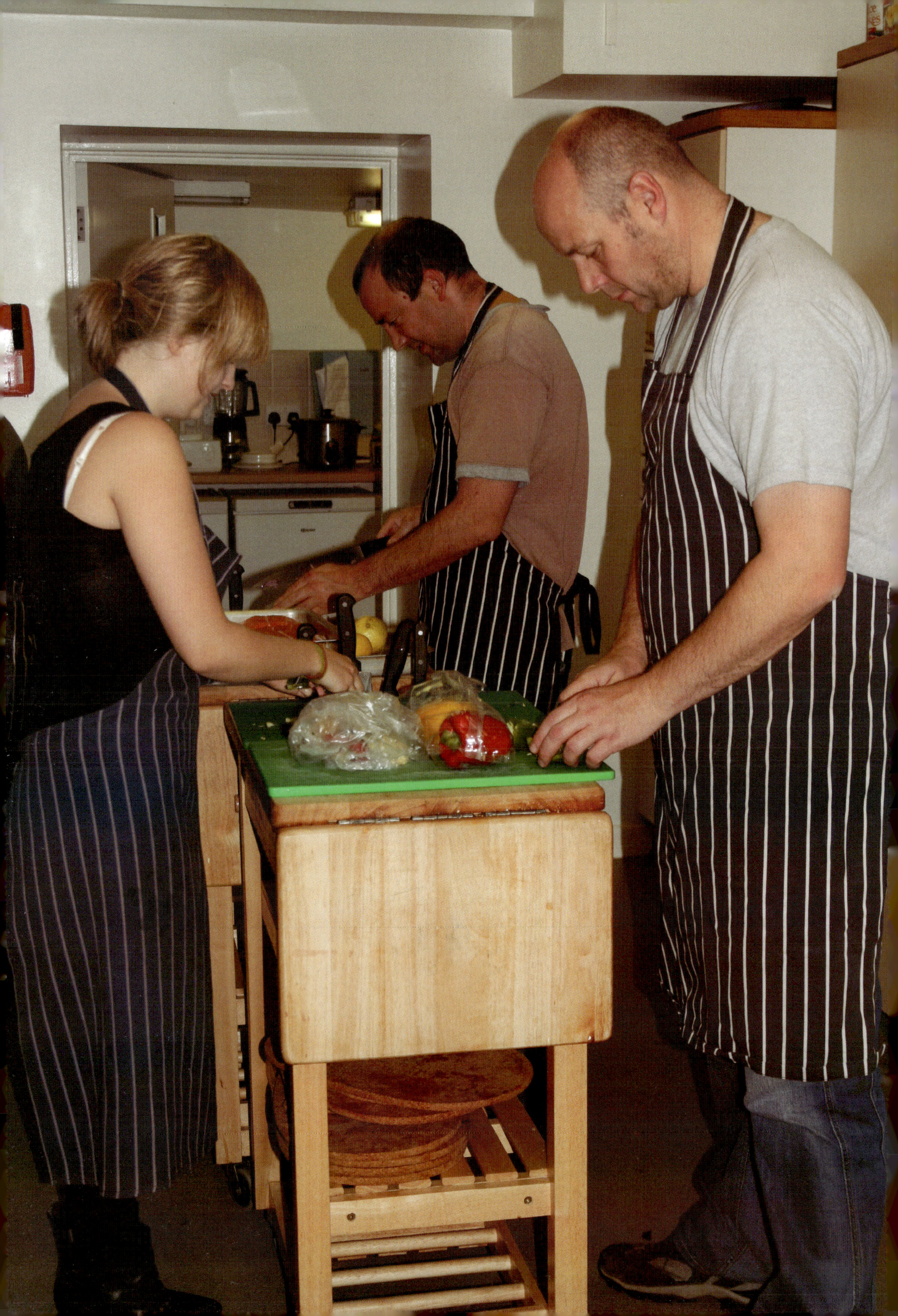

THE WRITERS' RECIPES

The cooking is a fun and important part of the Arvon experience - the preparing and sharing of food and ideas. Many participants talk fondly about this uniquely collective, creative spirit of the courses, and the chemistry of living and working with people from all walks of life. It is something they carry with them after the course has ended.

Since The Hurst first opened the menus have adapted to current fashions, local produce and food sensitivities. If you wished to re-create a particular menu, here are some genuine examples with the days of the week on which they appeared. Additional recipes which may have featured from time to time have also been included.

They are as cooked and eaten by the writers during their courses. They can recapture the spirit of their week at The Hurst and use the recipes at home for entertaining literary friends or book groups. To preserve something of that experience, I have kept the original quantities for 15 or more. They can easily be scaled down to more modest literary soirees. The quantities for the special dietary requirements are, of course, smaller.

"Evening meals are an integral part of the whole experience, as a group we cooked and ate together and as a result I've made new friends and contacts. They continue to encourage me having returned to the harsh realities of everyday life!" Colin Bell

HURST MENU

Tuesday

Crispy Skinned Chicken with Sweet Tomatoes
Leek, Courgette & Lentil au Gratin
Rice
Green Salad

Marmalade Bread and Butter Pudding

Wednesday

Spinach and Ricotta Lasagne
Green Salad

Fruit Crumble

Thursday

Salmon Steaks
Chick pea & spinach stew
Roasted Mediterranean Vegetables
Couscous

Fruit salad

Friday

Aromatic Lamb & Lentil Stew
Chilli Con Veggie
Mashed Potato
Red Pepper, Green Bean and Sesame Salad

Saucy Chocolate Pudding

Cottage Pie
Orange & honey chicken - like a simple tagine
Caribbean Baked Bananas

Cottage Pie

3 kg Minced Beef
6 Onions
8 Carrots
4 Cloves of Garlic
4 tablespoons of tomato ketchup (trust us)
8 teaspoons Worcestershire sauce
6kg Potatoes
Beef Stock

Preheat the oven to 200c
Step one: The Mashed Potatoes
You should do the potatoes early on as there is a lot of peeling to do and it doesn't matter if the mash goes cold – it's going back in the oven.
- Peel the potatoes
- chop the potatoes into roughly regular sizes and place them in a large saucepan
- Pour boiling water from the kettles over the potatoes, put the heat on the hob to high, and boil for 20 minutes or until a fork goes easily to the centre of the largest piece of potato
- Drain potatoes by pouring into a colander over a sink, return to the empty saucepan, and add butter and milk
- Mash until smooth and lump free

Step Two: The Meat
- Chop the onions and garlic and finely dice the carrots
- Heat the olive oil in a large saucepan.
- Add onions, garlic and carrots to the oil, and sweat them down in the saucepan (medium heat) until the onions have just started to brown and the carrots softened
- Add the meat and fry gently until it has browned nicely
- Add the ketchup and the Worcestershire sauce and stir in a cup of stock – add more stock if the mixture looks too dry, it should be well lubricated but not soupy
- Add salt and pepper and simmer for 30 minutes
- After 30 minutes, if meat is sloppy, add Bisto gravy granules if you like (optional)

Step Three: Assembly
Pour the meat into the two large metal baking trays (the ones with the handles) pile the mash evenly on top
Use a fork to spread the mash evenly over the meat and then rough up the surface
Bake in the oven for about 30 minutes until the mash is just browned

Salmon Steaks & Couscous

20 salmon steaks
5 lemons

1 kg couscous
2 litres hot vegetable stock (use Kallo Vegetable stock cubes)

Preheat oven to 200 C

The Salmon:
Wash and pat dry salmon steaks before spreading them out on two shallow baking trays. Drizzle with olive and season with salt and pepper before placing a thin slice of lemon on each.

Bake for approx 25 minutes.

Couscous

1 kg couscous
2 litres boiling water
4 x Kallo vegetable stock cubes
100g butter
Freshly ground black pepper
Fresh herbs of your choice, and/or pumpkin seeds, raisins, pine nuts, etc.

Start to prepare the couscous about ten minutes before you are ready to serve the food so that it remains hot.

First make stock. Pour one litre of boiling water into a large jug.
In a second jug, place 2 x Kallo stock cubes. Put a small amount of the boiling water from the first jug in with the stock cubes, and crush them with a spoon until they have fully dissolved. Add the rest of the water from the first jug. Do this a second time, with 2 x stock cubes and 1 litre of boiling water, in a third jug, so that you have two litres of stock.

Prepare and chop herbs, if using, and any other ingredients you want to add

Empty couscous packets into two large bowls. Pour half the stock over each bowl of couscous, and stir it in with a fork.

Cover the bowl with a lid, and leave it for 5 minutes to 'cook'.

Stir in butter (half in each bowl), pepper and any herbs or spices that you have prepared – couscous is very versatile.

Crispy Skinned Chicken with Sweet Tomatoes

20 chicken pieces
Sea salt
freshly ground black pepper
2 bunches of fresh basil,
6 punnets of cherry tomatoes, halved
1.5kg large tomatoes, quartered
6 yellow peppers, sliced
3 whole bulbs of garlic
3 fresh red chilli, finely chopped
Olive oil

Preheat the oven to 180c
STEP 1:
- Pick the leaves off the basil, then chop the stalks finely.
- Cut cherry tomatoes in half and large

tomatoes in quarters.
- Chop yellow peppers.
- Break garlic into cloves.
- Finely chop red chilli, taking care not to touch anything (especially your own face) and to thoroughly wash hands and wash chopping board & knife afterwards.

STEP 2:

Sprinkle the **chicken** pieces on all sides with salt and black pepper, and as you do, lay them in two large metal baking trays, in one snug-fitting layer. If they don't all fit, put the extra pieces in a smaller separate white ceramic dish.

Scatter the **basil** leaves and stalks evenly over the chicken pieces, then chuck in your **tomatoes & peppers,** making sure they are evenly spread over each dish.

Next scatter the **garlic** cloves and chopped **chilli** over each dish, and drizzle some **olive oil** over each piece of chicken. Mix around a bit, pushing some tomatoes & peppers underneath the chicken with a large spoon where you can.

Place in the oven for 1 1/2 hours. About half way through, take the trays out one by one, and carefully turn the tomatoes & peppers over with a spoon, then return tp oven.

STEP 3:

Test the chicken to see if it is thoroughly cooked before serving.

To do this, firstly, look at the chicken and see if the skin is crisp. Next, take one tray of chicken out of the oven, and stick a fork into the thickest part of the biggest piece of chicken, sticking it in all the way to the bone, and wiggle it round. If the meat falls easily off the bone when you do this, it is cooked. If it doesn't fall away from the bone, put the chicken back in the oven for another ten minutes, then test it again before serving.

Orange & Honey Chicken

20 chicken pieces
1 jar runny honey
10 oranges

Preheat the oven to 200 C

Chicken:
Slice half the oranges (there should be one slice per chicken piece) and put them on the two flat metal roasting trays.

Arrange the chicken pieces on top of the orange slices.

Drizzle the chicken with olive oil; then honey.

Squeeze the juice from the other half of the oranges and pour over the chicken.

Roast in the oven for 1 hour and 10 minutes AND pierce with a knife to check that the juices run clear to be certain that it is done.

Vegetarian Cottage Pie

250g lentils
3 Onions
4 Carrots
2 Cloves of Garlic
2 tablespoons of tomato ketchup
4 teaspoons marmite
2 kg Potatoes
Vegetable Stock

Preheat the oven to 200C

The Filling: Place the lentils in a saucepan and cover with boiling vegetable stock. Boil for 30 minutes or until the lentils soften.

Meanwhile heat the olive oil in a large saucepan. Chop the onions and garlic and finely dice the carrots and then sweat them down in the saucepan (medium heat) until the onions have just started to brown and the carrots softened. Add the lentils and fry gently for a few minutes. Next add the wine, the ketchup and the Worcestershire sauce and stir in a cup or two of stock – add more stock if the mixture looks too dry, it should be well lubricated but not soupy. Add salt and pepper and simmer for 30 minutes.

The Mashed Potatoes: You should do the potatoes early on as there is a lot of peeling to do and it doesn't matter if the mash goes cold- it's going back in the oven. Peel the potatoes, chop them into roughly regular sizes and place them in a large saucepan. Pour boiling water from the kettles over the potatoes and boil for 20 minutes or until soft enough to mash. Drain, return to the saucepan, add butter and milk and then mash until smooth and lump free.

Assembly: Pour the filling into a green casserole pot and then pile the mash on top. Use a fork to spread the mash evenly over the meat and then rough up the surface. Bake in the oven for about 30 minutes until the mash is just browned.

Roasted Mediterranean Vegetables

Bunch fresh rosemary
10 courgettes
3 aubergines
5 red onions
12 peppers (4 green, 4 red, 4 yellow)
2 heads garlic

Olive Oil

Preheat the oven to 200 C

Cut up the vegetables and place into two deep metal baking dishes – the ones with the handles. Don't cut them too small as chunky vegetables roast better.

Baste with olive oil, season with salt and pepper and throw in whole cloves of garlic – no need to peel them.

Place bunches of rosemary in each dish and roast in the oven for 1 hour.

Leek, Courgette & Lentil Au Gratin

2 Onions
8 tablespoons butter or margarine
2 cups red split lentils
3 1/2 cups water or veggie stock
2 Bay leaves
juice of 1 lemon
sea salt
freshly ground black pepper
4 leeks
2 courgettes
fresh herbs
grated cheese (optional)

Preheat the oven to 190C

Wash the lentils in cold water and drain them. Fry the onion in 4 tablespoons of margarine in a medium sized saucepan for 5 minutes, and then add the lentils and the water or stock, and bay leaves. Simmer them on low for 20-30 minutes, until the lentils are soft and golden-beige.

Remove the bay leaves and put the lentil mixture plus the lemon juice, salt and pepper in the blender and whizz.

Wash and trim the leeks, and slice finely. Chop the courgettes into chunks. Fry courgettes and leeks in 3 tablespoons of butter until golden. Remove from the pan with a slotted spoon.

Use the remaining margarine to grease an ovenproof dish. Spread the cooked leeks and courgettes out in the dish and pour the lentil mixture over the top. Sprinkle grated cheese and fresh herbs over the top.

Bake for 40 minutes.

Chickpea and Spinach Stew

To serve 4

2 tbsp olive oil
1 red onion, finely sliced
3 garlic cloves, finely sliced
2 teaspoons freshly grated ginger
1 red or yellow pepper
1 tsp sea salt
2 x 400g tins of chickpeas, drained
80ml/2½fl oz water
1 tsp cumin
1 tsp turmeric, optional
freshly ground black pepper
500g tomatoes, chopped
100g spinach leaves

Heat a large pot over a high heat.

Add oil, onion, garlic, ginger, peppers and salt and cook for five minutes (or until the onions are soft) being careful to stir regularly.

Add the chickpeas, 80ml water, cumin, turmeric and black pepper to taste and cook for five minutes or until the water evaporates.

Add the chopped tomatoes and cook for another two minutes to soften.

Remove from the heat and taste to check for seasoning. Stir through the spinach.

Serve with yoghurt and rice or couscous.

Aromatic Lamb & Lentil Stew

6 lb cubed lamb
1.5 litres boiling water (from kettles)
7 x Kallo Organic Chicken Stock Cubes
1.5 kg canned chopped tomatoes
400g red lentils
8 tbls olive oil

SPICES:
4 teaspoons cumin
2 teaspoons turmeric
10 cardamom pods (bruised)
1 cinnamon stick
3 star anise
8 whole cloves

Put large pot on hot plate, and when it's hot add the oil and brown the lamb in batches. Return all the lamb to the pot and add all other ingredients. Bring back to the boil.

Simmer at medium heat (it should be bubbling but not boiling over) for 2 hours, stirring occasionally to ensure the lentils don't stick to the bottom of the pan.

Serve with rice and yoghurt. (Yoghurt can be mixed with dried mint if you like.)

Chilli Con Veggie

1 1/2 lb onions
1 head garlic
1 lb mushrooms
2 lb courgettes
6 peppers
4 tins tomatoes
3 tins kidney beans (2.5 kilo)
Tomato puree
Salt
2 Bay Leaves
2 Teaspoons sugar
2 Teaspoons Cumin
Paprika
Chilli powder

METHOD:

Heat some oil in a large pan and gently fry half the chopped onions and half the garlic. Add the rest of the vegetables and stir until sweated.

Add 4 tins of tomatoes, 3 tins of kidney beans, a teaspoon of salt, 2 bay leaves, 2 teaspoons of sugar, a glass of red wine, 2 teaspoons of cumin and paprika and 2 (or more to taste) teaspoons of chilli powder. Add half a tube of tomato puree, cover and simmer for 1 1/2 hours (or longer).

Red Pepper, Green Bean & Sesame Salad

8 red peppers
1 kg green beans
2 Garlic heads
1 cup vegetable oil
2 cups water
6 tablespoons Sesame oil
4 teaspoons salt
2 teaspoons white sugar
1/2 cup sesame seeds

The Vegetables:

Prepare the vegetables by thinly slicing red peppers into long strips and top'n'tailing green beans. Chop garlic finely.

Heat a large pot and when hot add 1/2 cup vegetable oil. When oil is hot add garlic, stir a couple of times until it is sizzling, then add all the vegetables.
Keep the pot on high heat for about 5 minutes, turning the vegetables often.

Sprinkle over salt, sugar, water and sesame oil. Turn heat to low, cover pot with lid, and let simmer for 5 minutes.

When cooked but still crispy (bite a bean to see), take off the heat. Lift vegetables onto flat square plates with tongs (i.e. draining off excess liquid). Let cool to room temperature. Sprinkle with sesame seeds and extra sesame oil. Serve.

Spinach and Ricotta Lasagne

The Sauce:
6 pints of milk
250g butter
300g plain flour
3 bay leaves (pick from bay trees)
250g Parmesan (grated)

The Lasagne:
2.5 kg spinach
1kg ricotta
Lasagne sheets
1 tsp nutmeg
600g Shropshire Blue (chopped)
600g Mozzarella (grated)

Preheat the oven to 180C

Preparing: Grate the mozzarella and parmesan, keeping them separate from each other. Chop the Shropshire Blue into walnut sized pieces.

The Sauce: Place a large saucepan over a medium/high heat. Melt butter, mix in flour with a whisk, and gradually whisk in milk which has been pre-heated to almost boiling point in the microwave. Add bay leaves and season with salt and pepper. Stir with whisk continually on a high heat until it comes to simmering point and has thickened.

Remove from the heat and stir in about $3/4$ (NOT ALL) of the grated Parmesan. Discard the bay leaves and cover the sauce with cling film to prevent a skin from forming.

The Spinach: Wash all the spinach really thoroughly and shake dry. Place a knob of butter in one of the large saucepans and add the spinach with a sprinkle of salt. Place the pan over a medium heat and add spinach to it in batches, turning over continuously, until the leaves have collapsed. If after all spinach has been added the leaves have not wilted, put a lid on the pan and turn the heat to low and leave for 2-3 minutes, turning the spinach every minute until it has all wilted. Drain the spinach is a colander and squeeze out as much moisture as you can by pressing a plate down onto the leaves.

Next, chop the spinach and place in a large mixing bowl with the ricotta and about 150ml of the sauce. Add the nutmeg, salt and pepper and stir well.

Assembling: Take the two deep metal baking trays (the ones with handles) and grease with butter. Spread about one quarter of the sauce on the bottom of the two trays and then a third of the spinach mixture. Place a layer of pasta sheets over this and then repeat the whole process, this time adding a third of the grated mozzarella and the chopped Shropshire blue. Add a second layer of pasta and repeat. Finish with a layer of pasta topped with the rest of the sauce and the remaining Parmesan and mozzarella.

Cooking: Place the lasagne in the pre-heated oven and bake for 50-60 minutes or until the top is golden and bubbling. Remove from the oven and let settle for 10 minutes before serving. Serve: with salad.

What's in a name?

Shropshire Blue, often described as 'an orange Stilton,' has travelled well. It started life as Inverness Blue or Blue Stuart but first took off when re-named Shropshire Blue. However, despite the name, it was still being made outside the county in Cheshire and Nottinghamshire. When the name and goodwill were sold on the manufacture of the cheese was taken over by the Long Clawson and Colston Bassett dairies.

This was too much for our patriotic cheesemakers. Finally Shropshire has the blues; Ludlow Blue is made by the Ludlow Food Centre, Wrekin Blue in Newport, and Marches Blue in Oswestry.

Dairy Free/Gluten Free Lasagne

Gluten Free Lasagna Sheets
1 Jar Napoli Sauce
or much nicer with homemade Napoli**

Salt, pepper, fresh herbs from garden (oregano, chives, thyme, marjoram)

Dairy free cream/soy yoghurt

Prepared/Cooked Vegetables such as:
- Spinach - wilted and chopped, can be mixed with dairy free yoghurt for a creamy layer
- sweet potato or squash, sliced thinly and roasted on a tray in a 200 degree oven for 20 minutes until soft, or
- courgettes (sliced thinly & fried in olive oil), or
- Red peppers (roasted and peeled)

(or combination of the above, a good mix is a layer of sweet potato, one layer spinach etc)

Preheat the oven to 180C

Layer the vegetables, Napoli sauce, herbs, seasoning & lasagne sheets (including dairy free cheese, or dairy free yoghurt, if using).

The last layer should be lasagne sheets topped with enough sauce to cover the pasta and a sprinkling of fresh herbs.

Top with Napoli sauce and soy yoghurt. Sprinkle with dairy free cheese, if using.

Bake for 50 minutes.

** Homemade Napoli sauce

Fry 2-3 cloves of garlic (chopped) in olive oil for one minute, add chopped canned tomatoes. Add one or two vegetarian Kallo gluten free/dairy free stock cubes. Add herbs. Simmer until tasty and slightly thickened.

Marmalade Bread and Butter Pudding

One loaf of sliced white bread
Butter
Marmalade
1 teaspoon of cinnamon or nutmeg
Half a mug of sugar
Raisins
4 eggs
1 pint milk
1 pint cream
Preheat the oven to 200C

Lightly butter a white ceramic baking dish.

Butter and marmalade all the slices of bread and cut in half diagonally (triangles).

In a large bowl whisk together the cream, milk, cinnamon, sugar and eggs.

Arrange one layer of bread over the base of the baking dish and sprinkle with raisins. Add another layer of bread and then another of raisins and repeat until there is no bread left.

Pour the milk and cream mixture over the bread and sprinkle with the top brown sugar.

Put in the oven for 35 minutes or until the top is golden brown.

Easy Peasy Trifle for Adults

Ingredients:

24 Boudoir Biscuits
A sprinkle of Brandy or Rum
2 cups chopped fruit (oranges, melon etc) soaked in 1 cup orange juice (or 2 x cans fruit)
1 bunch grapes
4 bananas
1-2 litres of ready-to-serve custard
Whipped cream (whip fresh cream with icing sugar to taste) or canned spray cream
Sprinkles

Method:

- Chop fruit and soak in 1 cup of orange juice.
- Take a white ceramic baking dish and make a layer of boudoir biscuits on the bottom.
- Sprinkle boudoir biscuits with brandy or rum, then cover in chopped fruit and sprinkle in the fruit's soaking juice.
- Cut grapes in half and slice bananas – spoon the grapes and the bananas over the biscuits

- Pour the custard over the fruit – you don't have to use all the custard, make sure you leave room for the cream on top. Use 1 litre plus a little more if necessary.
- Cover in cling film and place in fridge for at least 1 hour (i.e. 6.30pm at the latest).
- Whip cream with electric hand beater until thick & sweeten with sifted icing sugar if liked (or if using spray cream, shake can).
- Just before serving cover in cream and sprinkle sprinkles on top

Fruit Crumble

300g plain flour
250g sugar
250g butter (soft)
1.5 kg pie fruit (e.g. apple, or apple and rhubarb)
1 lemon (juice and rind)
1 teaspoon cinnamon (if apple)

Preheat the oven to 180 C

Place sliced (and peeled if appropriate) fruit into a buttered white ceramic baking dish, sprinkle with sugar, lemon juice, lemon rind and cinnamon (if apple).

Blend the sugar, flour and butter together either in the food processor or by hand until the texture is that of fine crumbs.

Spread evenly over the fruit and bake in the oven for 30 minutes or until golden brown.

Serve with cream or ice cream.

Caribbean Baked Bananas

20 bananas
10 tablespoons of rum
250g raisins
12 tablespoons brown sugar
1 lemon (juice and zest)
1 orange (juice and zest)

METHOD:

Preheat the oven to 180 C

Place the raisins in a small bowl, cover with the rum and leave to soak while you prepare the bananas.

Peel and slice the bananas into thick slices (about 1.5 inches). Butter one of the white porcelain oven dishes and sprinkle half the sugar over the base. Arrange the bananas on top of the sugar and pour over the rum and raisins followed by the orange and lemon zest and juice. Sprinkle over the remaining sugar and cover with tin foil.

Bake in the oven for 30 minutes, removing the foil for the last 5 minutes.

Serve with ice cream.

Saucy Chocolate Pudding

6 oz sugar
6 oz fine semolina
3 oz cocoa powder
2 1/2 tablespoons baking powder
3 oz butter (melted)
6 eggs (beaten)
3 drops vanilla essence

1/2 lb light brown sugar
5 tablespoons cocoa powder
1 1/4 pints hot water

The Pudding

Pre-heat the oven to 180 C

Mix the sugar and semolina together in a large bowl. Add the cocoa powder and the baking powder and mix thoroughly.

In a separate bowl, whisk together the melted butter, eggs and vanilla essence. Add this to the dry ingredients and mix well. Pour the mixture into a buttered white ceramic dish.

The Sauce Mix the brown sugar and cocoa powder together and gradually stir in the hot water. Pour the mixture over the pudding and then bake in the oven for 45 minutes, or until the liquid has sunk to the bottom and the sponge is well risen and springy.

Serve with ice cream or cream.

LUNCHES

Lunch at The Hurst is another chance to explore the local foods in season – salads, fruits, cheeses and a variety of loaves. Ruth Mason is the regular cook who has made quiches and pates her speciality. She can meet any dietary need.

Ruth's Quiches

Writers are a mixed bunch and many have dietary requirements, so I've devised these recipes to meet as many as feasible without having to produce separate meals. Arvon is all about being inclusive and that's reflected here.

Gluten and/or dairy free needs (or choices) are much more usual now, as are vegetarian and vegan diets.

Initially I used commercial Gluten Free (GF) flour products suitable for pastry. They produced a slightly rubbery pastry that kind of "squeaks" on the teeth, so I experimented by adding 1 part cornmeal to 5 parts GF flour. This opened up the texture and overcame the chewiness but it was still a little more like eating the packaging than the pastry. Then I found a GF flour mix recipe that doesn't have Xanthum gum (for malleability) but still works – in fact it works very well.

Like all GF pastry, rolling it out is difficult. I've rolled GF pastry between two sheets of clingfilm with some success, using the clingfilm to help move it. But it cracks, flops and looks pretty rustic. This GF pastry makes a terrific quiche base if you press it gently into the base of the tin. It handles like shortbread so don't try to do the sides. You can still slice and serve it like regular quiche so long as you run a knife around the edge first.

Gluten Free Flour
(equivalent to Plain or All-Purpose flour)
    3 parts cornmeal (fine or medium)
    5 parts rice flour (brown for flavour)
    2 parts cornflour

Mix well and store in an airtight container. Make a batch and use as required.

GF Vegan Pastry
(makes 1x12"/30cm Quiche)
    500g GF flour
    230g Dairy-free margarine
    ¼ tsp salt
    Cold water

1. Rub fat into sifted flour & salt with fingertips until it resembles fine breadcrumbs. (21st Century folk can pulse it gently in a food processor.)
2. Gradually add water a tbsp at a time, mixing with the flat blade of a knife until it forms a soft ball of dough.
3. Wrap the lump of dough in a bag or clingfilm and refrigerate for 30 minutes. This is important, as GF flours take longer than wheat flours to absorb water. The dough will be firmer when you come to use it and less likely to crack when cooked

Vegetarian Dairy-Free Quiche
(1x12"/30cm Quiche)
    6 Medium eggs (free-range and local)
    100ml Soy milk or similar
100g Vegetarian Cheese, grated (omit or replace with fully Dairy Free equivalent if required)
    Enough seasonal vegetables to scatter over the base
    1 quantity of GF Vegan Pastry

1. Heat the oven to 190°C/375°F, Gas 5, Aga Hot-oven
2. Use a pizza pan or similar. A loose-bottomed pan is not suitable, as this quiche has no sides to contain the filling. Gently press the pastry evenly into the pan, ensuring no cracks are left.
3. Scatter the vegetables, followed by the cheese, evenly over the base.
4. Whisk the eggs and milk and pour into the quiche.
5. Season with salt and generous black pepper
6. Cook for 25-35 minutes, until set to a very slight wobble and golden-brown
7. Rest until the filling deflates, run a knife around the edge, slice, and serve.

NOTES: What veg you use is your choice, but most will need pre-cooking before going into the quiche. Steam, boil, blanche, or microwave fresh green veg, except spinach, which can go in fresh. Onions, tomatoes, peppers, and mushrooms have a better flavour if roasted for a few minutes or softened by frying. Courgettes and aubergines look better if slightly browned by grilling or frying.

Vegan Quiche
(1x12"/30cm Quiche)
    1 quantity of GF Vegan Pastry
    Seasoning
    Base Filling (this forms the body of the quiche like the eggs in a non-vegan version)
    Toppings

1. Heat the oven to 190°C/375°F, Gas 5,

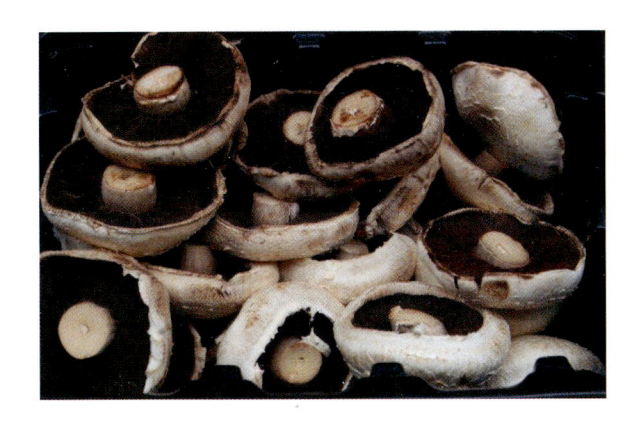

Aga Hot-oven
2. Use a pizza pan or similar. A loose-bottomed pan is not suitable as this quiche has no sides to contain the filling. Gently press the pastry evenly into the pan, ensuring no cracks are left.
3. Spread the Base Filling over the pastry to a depth of about half the pan.
4. Arrange the toppings, pressing gently into the filling.
5. Season well
6. Cook for 25 minutes until pastry is cooked and the top browned
7. Loosen, slice, and serve.

Notes:
Base Filling suggestions:
    Roasted squash, mashed
    Hummus
    Chestnut Puree
    Cooked lentils
    Cooked sweet-potato, mashed
    Roasted parsnip, mashed

The Filling should be spreadable and soft enough to allow for some drying-out as the pastry cooks, but it should hold together as the quiche is served.
Topping suggestions:
    Roasted Mediterranean vegetables
    Sliced Mushrooms
    Caramelised Onions
    Cherry Tomatoes

Choose toppings to compliment the Filling, and take some care when arranging.
A sprinkle of roasted seeds or nuts adds an interesting crunch.

TEATIME

Lucky visitors if a tutor or writer has a birthday whilst at The Hurst. For then a Carys Palmer Celebration cake will appear - using the finest local ingredients and decorated with handmade sugar decorations, or edible pictures.

Reading and other Sources

A Taste of Clun	Clun Memorial Hall
Clun Valley Sampler	Clun Memorial Hall
Eliza Acton	The Best of Eliza Acton
Mrs Beeton's	Family Cookery
Carol Bowen	The Country Range Cook Book
Peter Brears	Traditional Food in Shropshire
Collins Gem	Food for Free
Elizabeth David	Italian Food
Elizabeth David	Classics of Mediterranean Food, French Country Cooking and Summer Cooking
Jane Grigson	English Food, Good Things, Fish Cookery
Dorothy Hartley	The Land of England, Food in England
John Heilpern	John Osborne A Patriot for Us
Jocasta Innes	The Pauper's Cook Book
Bee Nilson	The Penguin Cookery Book
Jennifer Patterson	Seasonal Recipes
Meg Pybus	Under the Buttercross
Meg & Keith Pybus	Eat The View
Gary Rhodes	Rhodes around Britain
Karen Wallace	Shropshire Food
Mary Webb	Golden Arrow
Florence White	Good Things in England
V. Sackville West	The Land

Recipe Index

Beef Casserole in the Orchard	54
Beetroot & Orange Soup	33
Blackberry & Apple Dumplings	50
Blackcurrant Gooseberry Snow	41
Bonfire Toffee Apples	50
Boozy Bananas	35
Caribbean Baked Bananas	86
Chicken Breasts in Ginger Wine	32
Chicken Crispy Skinned Sweet Tomatoes	77
Chicken Orange & Honey	78
Chickpea and Spinach Stew	81
Chilli Con Veggie	82
Christmas Ham	56
Clive of India's Apple Chutney	46
Cottage Pie	76
Cottage Pie Vegetarian	79
Damson Sauce	49
Duckling with Honey Roast	38
Easy Peasy Trifle	85
Elderflower Cheesecake	64
Elderflower Cordial	65
Fruit Crumble	86
Hazelnut Brownies	68
Hedgerow Jelly	71
Helen's Fish Cakes	54
Kerry's Wild Strawberry Jam	67
Lamb & Lentil Aromatic Stew	81
Lamb Provençale Leg	31
Lasagne Dairy Free/Gluten Free	84
Leek, Courgette & Lentil Au Gratin	80
Little Orange Custard Pots	55
Marmalade Bread and Butter Pudding	84
Mediterranean Vegetables Roasted	80
Mushrooms and Chicken Livers	63
Nettle and Wild Garlic Soup	61
Old Mother Osborne's Tomato Ketchup	39
Pheasant with Juniper & Apple	47
Potato Latkes	55
Puffballs Fried	68
Quiches – Ruth's	87-89
Gluten Free Flour	
GF Vegan Pastry	
Vegan	
Vegetarian Dairy-Free	
Red Cabbage	48
Rhubarb Fool	34
Rowan Berry Jelly	67
Salmon En Papillote	40
Salmon Steaks & Couscous	76/77
Saucy Chocolate Pudding	87
Savoury Meatballs	39
Shropshire Fitchet Pie	48
Sloe Gin	69
Spinach and Ricotta Lasagne	83
Trout from the River Clun	33
Veggie Magic	40
Venison steaks with Port	48
Virgin Mint Julep	35
Wimberry Clafoutis	65
Wimbledon Sorbet	41
Wine Jelly	56

Dear Readers,

Creating a book is like having a baby...

It isn't just the research, the writing, the conversion of pounds to kilos, cups to fl. ozs and centimetres to furlongs, when you take on the whole project then you're with it to the end – before it goes to the printer, you'll have read every page a dozen times and you'll struggle to spot the typos.

And then there are the blessed 'widows' (words at the end or beginning of paragraphs left to sit alone) which you are supposed to hunt down.

I once wrote and virtually self-published a book which involved me in a weekly round trip of 60 miles to the designers and printers. Now that my clock is further advanced than the distance, there would have been no baby, and John Osborne would not have been entertained, let alone amused, if I had not had help closer to hand.

When we chose to live at nearly 1,000ft up in the Shropshire Hills, we gave great thought to the services we might need as the years rolled on – the railway, the surgery, the shops and markets. I must admit we didn't give thought to a designer for another book.

People from more urban environments don't realise the strength of the creative services in this area. When the time came to translate three years of preparation into print I literally drove two miles down the road and there waiting for me on the Craven Arms Business Park was James Sherratt of Craven Design and Print Ltd.

Like having a baby, there are deadlines of course. We were committed to a major public launch and still had miles to go in terms of matching dozens and dozens of photographs to the texts. James said it would take us about two weeks once we started and he would set aside the time necessary to meet the deadline. He did and here we are on time and on budget.

This book has not had the smoothest of passages. When we reached the design stage, I had used up all my reserves for crises. I needed a calming influence – James is that in spades.

I am thrilled with the look of the book. If it succeeds we couldn't have made it without James, so, unless you're having a baby, in which case better stick to the NHS, give Craven Design and Print a try.

Meg Pybus

Meg

PS. They're also very green. You can call in and visit the recycling centre at the same time.

SHROPSHIRE HILLS FOOD AND DRINK

Shropshire Hills Farmers' Markets

There are a number of regular farmers' markets in the Shropshire Hills which offer a variety of seasonal produce. Make sure you don't miss out by marking them on your calendar. For more details regarding any of the markets please contact them directly.

Bishops Castle Farmers' Market

Town Hall and adjacent Market Square, Bishops Castle, Shropshire,
Bishop's Castle Farmers' Market is held on the third saturday of every month in the Town Hall and the adjacent Market Square. 9am to 2pm.

Craven Arms Farmers Market

Shropshire Hills Discovery Centre, Craven Arms, Shropshire,
A regular Farmers' Market on the 1st Saturday of every month based at the Shropshire Hills Discovery Centre.

Knighton Farmers Market

Knighton Community Centre, Knighton, Powys,
A twice monthly farmers' market, every second and fourth Saturday of the month which include a wide variety of food and drink producers as well as local craftspeople.

Much Wenlock Farmers Market

Guild Hall, Much Wenlock,
A small twice monthly market every first and third Friday of the month.

Ludlow Local Produce Market

Castle Square, Ludlow, Shropshire, SY8 1AS
A wide variety of meat produce is available including free range chicken and pork, organic mutton, locally smoked salmon, game from local farms and estates. Other produce include local beer, cheeses and yoghurt, honey, fruit and vegetables, apple juice and delicious cakes and sweets and lots more besides.

The Local to Ludlow campaign promotes food and drink produced within 30 miles of the town. Our aim is to reduce the environmental cost of food production and to support the local food economy.

- Organise Ludlow Local Produce Market in Castle Square on the second and fourth Thursday of every month.
- Promote and support local food and drink producers and shops and businesses that sell or use locally sourced materials in their products or meals.
- Teach cookery classes at local schools or community venues using a mobile kitchen trailer.
- Re-connect people with the land through farm visits and re-skilling local communities in growing and cooking their own food.
- Reduce our environmental impact by selling compostable jute shopping bags and cutting down on packaging and food miles.

http://www.localtoludlow.org.uk/

Shropshire Hills Food and Drink
and our Environment

By buying local products you support sustainable small scale farming and businesses which contribute to conserving and enhancing the environment. Use this website to search for local food and drink as well as places where you can eat, stay and enjoy local produce.

http://www.shropshirehills-buylocal.co.uk/

Friends of the Shropshire Hills

Share your love of the Shropshire Hills.

Friends of the Shropshire Hills aims to foster a sense of belonging and encourage more people to care about the landscape, and contribute to conserving and sustaining it.

Friends is a network which will appeal to a wide range of people with a common interest in this beautiful landscape, its wildlife, heritage, culture and well-being.

Joining is easy and only costs £5 for individual annual membership. All money goes towards supporting local projects.

http://www.shropshirehillsaonb.co.uk/friends.htm

THE ARVON FOUNDATION

The Arvon Foundation is a registered charity which strives to promote the transforming power of writing. Through public courses, partnerships and work with young people, Arvon has helped thousands of individuals to begin a creative journey of self-discovery and imagination through writing.

The Arvon Foundation sprang to life in 1968 as a reaction by two poets, John Moat and John Fairfax, to what they saw as a dogmatic and lifeless approach to teaching poetry. Their solution was to encourage young people to find their voices by removing them from their everyday lives and enabling them to live and work with two published writers for a week. The infectious energy and idealism of Moat and Fairfax took off and captured the imagination of young people, teachers and writers, laying the basis for what has become a thriving and prestigious national enterprise.

Today Arvon runs four historic writing houses in the UK, where published writers lead week-long residential courses with individuals at all stages of their writing lives. Public courses are offered in a diverse range of genres, from novel writing, advanced poetry and radio fiction to food writing and comedy. Many highly regarded writers have at one time attended an Arvon course: Andrew Motion, Hilary Mantel, Lemn Sissay, Pat Barker, Roger McGough, Alan Hollinghurst and Sian Hughes among them. No qualifications or previous experience are required; Arvon is for anyone with a desire to write.

Arvon's ongoing commitment to open access is reflected in its grants programme, which provides financial support to enable those on low or no income to attend a course. Young people remain a vital part of the organisation's work and hundreds of under-18s participate in bespoke courses every year. Partnerships with groups such as the Medical Foundation for the Care of Victims of Torture and The Princess Royal Carers Trust continue to bring a diverse range of writers to Arvon.

For more information about The Arvon Foundation see
www.arvonfoundation.org
The Arvon Foundation Ltd is a registered charity number No. 306694.

arvon

About the Authors

Meg Pybus's father was the regional fatstock officer for the West Midlands. She was raised on farms, in butchers' shops and abbatoirs. For ten years she grazed in the fields of Germany, Sweden and Benelux. All of which she has put to good use as a culinary historian. Her works include *Under the Buttercross Market Drayton a Town of Good Food (1986)*, *Shropshire in the Marches 1997* (interview with Sean Hill), *Eat the View* [South Shropshire Tourism Association 2004 with the support of The Countryside Agency – this was the first attempt to spread the gourmet reputation of Ludlow to the surrounding agricultural and market towns area], *Shropshire's Spicy Secrets* (history of gingerbread), research and creation of *Produce of the Severn Valley* (a group of specialist food producers around Bridgnorth), *South Shropshire 2005* (the first colour accommodation guide).

Gordon Dickins has been photographing Shropshire life and landscape for over 30 years. His photographic books include *Shropshire Seasons* (1993), *Quiet Mysteries* (1995) and *The Shropshire Hills* (1999). He is also the author of *An Illustrated Literary Guide to Shropshire* (1987) and co-author, with Gladys Mary Coles, of *Walks With Writers* (1992) and, with Keith Pybus, of *Market Drayton Then and Now* (1995) and *The Shropshire Hills* (2006 for the AONB).

Both have a track record of working with voluntary bodies and local organisations in the production of their books. Meg with the Drayton Civic Society and at all levels of tourism in Shropshire. Gordon was part of the successful Snailbeach community project which produced *Never on a Sunday* and is currently working on *Once Upon A Hill* [with Natural England] which will tell the story of the lead-miners and their cottages on the Stiperstones.

They are members of the Advisory Committee of The Hurst - The John Osborne Arvon Centre.